CHE GUEVARA THE CUBAN STYLE OF REVOLUTION VOL. 2

ABHILASH CHAUBEY

Contents

CHAPTER ONE

Che's Ideas about Imperialism and Socialism

C he silently resigned his cabinet post in Fidel Castro's government and disappeared from public view in 1965 (Deutschmann 1994:27–31). There was a great deal of speculation at the time about his disappearance. Some believed Che and Castro had had a serious disagreement and Che had been imprisoned or secretly executed. There were also reports that Che had been killed in the Dominican Republic during the civil war that took place there in the spring of 1965. Later on, there was speculation that Castro or elements within the Cuban regime had eliminated Che because of his opposition to certain policies advocated by the political faction within the Cuban Communist Party that believed Cuba should follow the advice of Cuba's advisors from the Soviet Union and the socialist Eastern European countries (such as Czechoslovakia, Poland, and East Germany) closely tied to the Soviet Union.

By the beginning of 1964, it was evident even to Che that his four-year plan initiated in 1961 to industrialize Cuba was having great diffi culties. He realized he and many of his comrades had underestimated the diffi culties involved in transforming Cuba from a largely agrarian economy dominated by the production and exportation of sugar into an industrialized economy based on the production of a wide range of agricultural as well as manufactured products and the extensive application of modern technology (Taibo 1996:482–500). He made Herculean efforts in his posts as head of the national bank and minister of industry. He worked 16–18 hours a day and drove those around him to do the same. He had a genius for fi nding innovative solutions to the country's problems associated with its lack of technology and the technical skills needed for industrial development. However, his exemplary leadership and commitment to his responsibilities and ideals could not overcome the many organizational defi ciencies, widespread lack of technology, shortage of replacement parts (caused largely by the U.S. economic blockade of Cuba), and the lack of trained cadres. All of these problems obstructed the expansion of both Cuba's agricultural production and the development of its underdeveloped manufacturing sector.

O n the basis of what Che told his friends, it is possible to ascertain what his thinking was during this period. In the fi rst place, it is clear that Che was forced to admit that Cuba would have to return to its historical mode of livelihood, that is, the production of sugar for export. Yet he was not willing to accept the advice of Cuba's Soviet and Eastern European advisors that the revolutionary government should abandon the goal of industrializing the country. He felt strongly that Cuba's economic relations with the socialist bloc of nations led by the Soviet Union should not be the same as those between capitalist countries. If Cuba could not industrialize by itself, as a result of its neocolonial legacy and the underdeveloped character of its economy, then, Che argued, the more developed socialist countries such as the Soviet Union had an obligation to help Cuba. He thought the Soviet Union should fi nance Cuba's longterm efforts to industrialize instead of expecting Cuba to serve primarily as the sugar mill for the socialist bloc.

C he found little sympathy for his ideas among the Soviet Union's leaders and the Soviet advisors in Cuba. They regarded his plans to industrialize Cuba as unrealistic and impractical. Even if Cuba were to succeed in transforming its economy with Soviet assistance, they argued that there would be an insuffi cient market for Cuba's manufactured goods. Moreover, they pointed out the island lacked most of the raw materials needed for heavy industries (Anderson 1997:488–89). They argued the size of Cuba's internal market was not large enough to make the production of its own manufactured items economically justifi able and that, in view of Cuba's political isolation, it could not expect to export manufactured products to any of its neighbors in the Western Hemisphere. When Che countered that Cuba would have an export market in Latin America as soon as the revolution was carried to other countries of Central and South America, the Soviets made it quite clear that they were not willing to risk basing their economic assistance to Cuba on this eventuality.

Che was also critical of the Soviet Union's state capitalist economic system and its reliance on what he regarded as basically capitalist methods of organization, management, and investment. In particular, Che felt that the Soviet system's reliance on material incentives and a system of decentralized fi nancial management in its state industries were contradictory to the development of a genuine socialist economy and the development of a socialist consciousness on the part of the workers (Gerassi 1968a:292–316). Moreover, he suspected Moscow and Washington had entered into a tacit agreement to respect each other's international spheres of infl uence, and as part of this agreement Moscow had promised to restrain Havana from promoting revolution throughout Latin America and the Caribbean.

Che felt strongly that Cuba should fi rmly align itself with the newly independent Third World nations of Africa, the Middle East, and Asia and assist national liberation struggles and socialist revolutions throughout the still colonized parts of the Third World. This idea motivated him to travel extensively throughout Africa and Asia during early 1965.

H e went on an extended state visit to Africa, China, and then back to Africa during the fi rst three months of 1965. In Africa, Che visited Algeria, Mali, Congo-Brazzaville, Guinea, Ghana, Dahomey (Benin), Tanzania, and Egypt, where he met with important African and Arab leaders such as presidents Ahmed Ben Bella of Algeria, Kwame Nkrumah of Ghana, Julius Nyerere of Tanzania, and Abdel Nasser of Egypt (Anderson 1997:620–21).

Che also made a trip to the People's Republic of China with the offi cial purpose of explaining Cuba's position with regard to the growing international confl ict between the Soviet Union and China. The Chinese were upset over what they considered to be Cuba's increasing support for the Soviet Union. Because of the growing tension between Cuba and China at the time, Che had only a brief, formal meeting with China's famous leader Mao Tse-tung, but he was able to meet at length with other top Chinese offi cials and discussed with them his ideas about a united anti-imperialist front to liberate the Third World from Western (U.S., British, French, Belgian, and Portuguese) imperialism.

Actually, Che's views were closer to those held at the time by the Chinese leadership than to the Soviet Union's, since he had become increasingly critical of the Soviet Union's international relations. He considered the course adopted by the Soviet Union under Premier Nikita Khrushchev to be a "rightist" deviation from socialism. He also considered the emphasis placed by the Soviet advisors in Cuba on continuing the country's specialization in sugar production, the use of material incentives to increase labor productivity, and allowing Cuba's state enterprises to adopt fi nancial self-management as contrary to the Cuban revolutionary regime's commitment to the rapid industrialization of the economy and the replacement of capitalist material incentives and methods of organization with communist moral incentives and methods of organization. He predicted (correctly as it turned out) the Soviet Union and the Soviet bloc of socialist countries would return to capitalism if they continued to rely on capitalist market mechanisms, material incentives, and enterprise self-management (Anderson 1997:697).

Following his visit to China, he returned to Africa via Paris, where he learned defi nitively of the death of his friend Masetti in Argentina and his abortive effort to start a guerrilla foco there. From Paris he fl ew to Dar es Salaam, Tanzania, where he met with President Nyerere and with the representatives in Dar es Salaam of the armed guerrilla movements fi ghting for national independence at that time in the Portuguese colonies of Angola and Mozambique, white-settler-controlled Rhodesia (Zimbabwe), and the former Belgian Congo (Taibo 1996:514–15). Among the representatives whom he met in Dar es Salaam were Gaston Soumaliot and Laurent Kabila, two of the leaders of the Congolese rebel movement that was then in control of the eastern portion of the Congo. Although he was not impressed by Soumaliot and most of the other representatives he met, he was favorably impressed by Kabila's leftist views, which he found similar to his own, and acting on the authority that he had previously received from Fidel Castro, Che offered to send to Kabila's forces Cuban arms and military advisors.

From Tanzania he went to Egypt, where he told President Nasser of his desire to go to the Congo at the head of the contingent of Cuban advisors he had promised Kabila. In February 1965, Che appeared as an observer at the second conference of the Organization of Afro-Asian Solidarity in Algeria, where he initiated a personal crusade to create an anti-imperialist front among the neutral nations of the Third World. In the speech he delivered at this conference, he criticized the socialist countries for being the "accomplices of imperialist exploitation" and called on them to support popular revolutions in the neocolonial and colonial countries of the Third World, instead of pursuing their own selfish foreign policy (Gerassi 1968:378–86).

T he Soviet observers who were in attendance were outraged. Following the conference, both Ben Bella of Algeria and Nasser of Egypt tried to talk Che out of the idea of heading a Cuban contingent to the Congo. Nasser warned him that if he went to the Congo he would be considered a white man and that his involvement there could only turn out badly (Taibo 1996:517). Ben Bella was more supportive and allowed Che to establish a base in the hills overlooking Algiers, which he and representatives of other Latin American revolutionary groups, supported by the Cuban government, used for training purposes and maintained as a sanctuary until Ben Bella was overthrown by a military coupe in June 1965.

When Che returned to Cuba in March 1965, he was ready to resign his position in the Cuban government in order to devote all his efforts to furthering the armed struggle against imperialism. Since he had played such an important role in the Cuban Revolution although not Cuban, he assumed be would be able to do the same elsewhere, not only in Latin America but this time in Africa.

S hortly after Che returned to Havana, he met with Fidel Castro to discuss the results of his travels and his views regarding the position Cuba should take in international affairs. At this meeting, it appears that Castro reproached Che for criticizing the Soviet Union and the other socialist countries in his speech at the Organization of Afro-Asian Solidarity in Algiers (Taibo 1996:522). Castro also made it clear that he was under both external and internal pressure to move Cuba closer to the Soviet Union in the growing split between the Soviet Union and revolutionary China. In fact, the Soviets and the old-guard members of the Cuban Communist Party within the Cuban regime were pressing him to come out openly in favor of the ideological position held by the leaders of the Soviet Union and against the more radical ideological line taken by the leaders of the People's Republic of China. These former allies were now locked in an international struggle for the leadership of the international socialist movement.

C he's radical brand of revolutionary socialist internationalism was not shared by the leadership of the Soviet Union and by the leaders of most of the pro-Soviet Communist parties in Latin America. The Soviet leadership regarded what they considered Che's radical leftist adventurism to be a threat to their own international strategy of peaceful competition and coexistence with the United States and its allies. However, there appears to have been some sympathy for Che among the Soviet leaders, especially since his infl uence had been decisive in convincing Fidel Castro to align Cuba with the Soviet Union shortly after the revolutionary government was formed in Cuba.

According to Feder Burlatsky, a former advisor to Soviet premier Khrushchev, the Soviet leadership disliked Che's revolutionary adventurism and they were afraid his example would lead the Cubans and other leftists in Latin America into taking actions that would provoke a major military confrontation between the Soviet Union and the United States (Anderson:581). But in an interview he gave to the journalist Jon Lee Anderson in 1995, Burlatsky claimed: "Even though Che was against our interests, there was still some sympathy for him. . . . There was a romantic aura around him; he reminded people of the Russian Revolution" (Anderson:581).

Anderson also interviewed Nikolai Metutsov, who was responsible for maintaining relations between the Communist Party of the Soviet Union and the Communist parties in the non-European socialist states such as Cuba and Vietnam. Metutsov told Anderson he "fell in love" with Che upon meeting him, because of his "very beautiful eyes," and because his stare was "so generous, so honest," and because he was impressed by the way he spoke with such impetus, "as if his words were squeezing you" (Anderson:585). According to Anderson, Metutsov's appraisal was that Che's views could not be easily classifi ed.

Externally one could truly say that, yes, Che Guevara was contaminated by Maoism because of his Maoist slogan that the rifl e can create power. And certainly he can be considered a Trotskyite because he went to Latin America to stimulate the revolutionary movement there . . . but in any case I think these are external signs, superfi cial ones, and that deep down, what was most profound in him was his aspiration to help man on the basis of Marxism-Leninism. (Anderson:585)

M etutsov told Anderson that he thought that Che's personal commitment to the cause of revolution was his "peculiarity." He said Che's dedication to armed struggle, while a source of worry for some members of the leadership of the Soviet Communist Party, was not perceived by the Soviet leadership as a whole to be a cause of signifi cant concern. Whether this last statement about their lack of concern was true is hard to assess now.

Che was committed to both fomenting revolution on a truly international scale and personally putting into practice his thesis that it was possible for a small, if committed, guerrilla force to ignite a full-scale popular revolution in countries under the control of oppressive regimes backed by U.S. imperialism. His so-called peculiar commitment to these beliefs was shared by most of his closest friends and comrades as well as many admirers and sympathizers around the world. His commitment threatened the positions of the pro-Soviet leaders of the orthodox Communist parties in Cuba and elsewhere as well as many other leftist political parties and governments not aligned with the Soviet Union. Che openly criticized these parties and movements for their unwillingness to fi ght U.S. imperialism and to engage in an armed revolution to bring down the capitalist regimes in their countries and build socialist societies in their place.

Che realized, however, Cuba had no other alternative but to side with the Soviet Union. Che also knew his continued presence in the government was a liability. This was because of several reasons: his disagreements with the Soviets over their ideological line and their foreign policy, Cuba's growing dependence on Soviet military aid and trade, and his desire to involve himself directly in the revolutionary struggles against imperialism taking place in Latin America and around the world.

He realized that it would be impossible for him to involve himself directly in a revolutionary struggle in Latin America or Africa if he continued to hold a high position in the Cuban government. The international repercussions would have been too great for Cuba. In view of these circumstances, Che decided to resign his positions in the Cuban government and leave Cuba. His main interest was carrying the revolution to South America, particularly his homeland Argentina. He had established ties with revolutionary groups throughout Latin America and in other parts of the world while he held his important positions in the Cuban government, and he now planned to use some of these connections to carry out his plans of taking an active leadership role in creating or aiding armed revolutionary movements in South America and Africa.

A. is friend and confi dant Fidel Castro encouraged him to go to Af-rica and assist the revolutionary movement in the Congo, since he felt the conditions were not yet ready for him to go to South America. Castro knew that he had become increasingly restless in his governmental posts in Cuba and was anxious to carry out what he considered to be his historic mission of liberating the Third World countries from Western imperialism and capitalist exploitation (Anderson 1997:628).

Of course, this meant resigning from his important positions in the Cuban government, and it meant leaving behind all that Che had accomplished in Cuba as well as his wife and fi ve children and most of his Cuban comrades (except for those who would accompany him fi rst to the Congo and later to Bolivia). It was an extremely diffi cult and courageous decision for him to make. However, Che was a man who was totally committed to carrying out his convictions. His wife, Aleida March, knew this well. She had learned this by his side during the revolutionary war against the Batista dictatorship, and she always knew that one day he would leave her and their children to fulfi ll his chosen destiny—to fi ght to the death if necessary against imperialism and for the establishment of socialism.

I. n her book about their life together (March 2008), she discusses the tremendous sacrifi ces they both endured as a result of his total commitment to live by his revolutionary ideals—ideals that she shared wholeheartedly with him. The separations were almost unbearable for both of them, since they never knew when or whether they would see each other again. ndeed, she tried repeatedly to convince him to take her with him—both on his mission to the Congo and to Bolivia. But he convinced her the time was not right for her to join him and their young children needed her to stay with them until they were much older.

Che was very close to his fi ve children even though they were very young when he left them—to his fi rst child Hildita (Hilda Beatriz Guevara Gadea), who lived with her mother (his fi rst wife, Hilda Gadea) in Havana, and to his four children with Aleida March: Aleida, Camilo, Celia, and Ernesto, who lived with him in Havana. He was also very much in love with Aleida. Therefore, his separation from Aleida and his children was very painful and he missed them deeply while he was in the Congo and Bolivia.

T he personal side of Che and his many admirable personal traits are revealed beautifully in Aleida March's book on their life together. She describes many intimate moments of touching tenderness and romantic love between them. In general, her account of their life together reveals both his continuing devotion to her and the sincere concern he always showed for her feelings and her personal welfare. During his long absences from Cuba, he would write love letters and poems for her and make tape recordings to be given to her and the children. In the letters and poems he wrote for her, he nearly always referred to her as *mi única,* (my only one), and they all display great affection and longing for her.

For example, here is a fragment of a poem he wrote for Aleida upon his departure for Bolivia (March 2008:221):

Adiós, my only one, do not tremble before the hungry wolves nor in the cold steppe of absence; by my heart I carry you and together we will continue until the road fades away . . .

And in the last message she received from him in Bolivia, he wrote the following:

My only one:

I am taking advantage of the trip of a friend to send you these words, which could go by mail, but a "semi-offi cial" road seems more intimate. I could tell you that I miss you to the point of losing sleep, but I know you would not believe me, so I will abstain.

But there are days in which the homesickness becomes uncontrollable and possesses me. On Christmas and New Years, above all, you don't know how much I miss your ritual tears, below a sky of new stars that remind me of how little of my life I have devoted to personal affairs. (March 2008:225)

In this last communication with his wife, one can sense his homesickness and longing for her as well as the sadness he felt over how little of his life he had spent with her and their children. He ended this message with a "kiss for the little pieces of fl esh [his children], all the rest" and a kiss for her that he said was "pregnant with sighs and anguish."

This romantic personal side of Che's life was little known to all but his inner circle of family and friends until Hilda Gadea published her book in the late seventies on her relationship with Che and more recently Aleida March published her book on their life together. In this regard, it is also important to recognize that the ideological cornerstone of Che's revolutionary thinking and practice was not guerrilla warfare or armed revolution but his almost utopian concept of *el hombre nuevo* (the new man or human being). He used this concept to express the almost spiritual belief he held in the development of new socialist human being for the 21st century. In fact, he believed the development of this new type of human being was an essential aspect of the construction of a genuine socialist society. His belief in this ideal human being was an important source of inspiration for him and for those who adopted or were infl uenced by his views on socialism and the future development of humanity (Siles del Valle 1996:47–92).

Che was dedicated to living his life in accordance with his ideal concept of the new type of human being that would come into existence in the revolutionary struggle to build a new socialist world order for humanity. Che believed this new type of human being would arise out of the revolutionary struggle to liberate humanity from the egoistic individualism, dehumanizing exploitation, and social alienation associated with capitalism.

C he felt the struggle against capitalism and the construction of a new socialist order required a new type of human being who would always be committed to making personal sacrifi ces for the good of others. Nowhere is this concept of *el hombre nuevo* presented more explicitly than in Che's essay "Socialism and Man in Cuba," written early in 1965 while he was traveling as a Cuban statesman in Africa. What follows are some brief excerpts from this essay (in Gerassi 1968:398–400).

H e describes the characteristics of revolutionary 21st-century men and women who he hoped would arise out of the struggle to build a socialist society. First and foremost, he believed they would be guided by "strong feelings of love" for humanity. He wrote:

Let me say, at the risk of appearing ridiculous, that the true revolutionary is guided by strong feelings of love. It is impossible to think of a true revolutionary without this quality.

While he felt that there could be "no life outside of the revolution" for the men and women of the new socialist society, he also believed the revolutionary leaders of the 21st century would have to avoid falling into "dogmatic extremes" and "have a highly developed sense of justice and truth." Thus, he wrote:

There is no life outside the revolution. In these conditions the revolutionary leaders must have a large dose of humanity, a large dose of a sense of justice and truth, to avoid falling into dogmatic extremes, into cold scholasticism, into isolation from the masses.

A s for the level of social commitment required of the new human being, he believed very strongly that this commitment would require a great deal of personal sacrifi ce. In this regard, he seems to have been writing as much about himself as the new socialist human being when he wrote the following lines:

E ach and every one of us punctually pays his share of sacrifi ce, aware of being rewarded by the satisfaction of fulfi lling our duty, aware of advancing with everyone toward the new human being who is to be glimpsed on the horizon.

Che fi rmly believed this ideal new human being would develop in the future, despite the diffi culties of achieving the level of social consciousness and social commitment required for this human development to take place. Thus, he wrote: "the road is long and in part unknown," but "we are aware of our limitations" and "we will make the twenty-fi rst century human being, we ourselves!"

H is widow, Aleida March, recounts in her book about their life together how Che's closest friends and comrades felt that he was the best example of the new human being he wrote and spoke about so frequently. As Fidel Castro says in his memoir of Che (Deutschmann 1994:108–9):

H e was a living example. It was his style to be the example, to set the example. He was a person with a great spirit of self-sacrifi ce, with a truly spartan nature, capable of any kind of self-denial. His policy was to set an example. We could say that his entire life was an example in every sphere. He was a person of absolute moral integrity, of remarkably fi rm principles, a complete revolutionary who looked toward the future, toward the humanity of the future, and who above all stressed human values, humanity's moral values. . . . None of the words I use about him involve the slightest exaggeration, the slightest overestimation. They simply describe the man we knew.

The Secret Mission in Africa

Fidel Castro supported Che's recommendations about providing Cuban support to the rebels in the Congo (later called Zaire), other liberation movements, and the new leftist governments in Africa. According to Castro, the rebels in the eastern Congo requested Cuban military assistance in 1964. In a 1987 interview with the Italian journalist Gianni Minà (Deutschmann 1994:118), which took place on the 20th anniversary of Che's death, Castro said the following about Che's involvement in the Congo:

At the time, white mercenaries had intervened in the former Belgian Congo, now Zaire. [President] Lumumba had been killed, a neocolonial regime was established, and a movement of armed struggle emerged in Zaire. We never made this public, but the revolutionary movement asked us for help and we sent instructors and combatants on an internationalist mission.

A. e also told Minà it was his idea that Che go with the Cuban force sent to the eastern Congo. In this regard, he said:

A. myself suggested the idea to Che. He had time on his hands, he had to wait [before the conditions were more favorable for his long-hoped-for mission to South America]. . . . So we put him in charge of the group that was going to help the revolutionaries in what is today Zaire. . . . n all, about 100 Cubans went and stayed there several months. He followed the approach of teaching Zairians how to fi ght. Cuban and Zairian patriots fought white mercenaries and the forces sent by the government. . . . In the end the revolutionary leaders of the former Belgian colony decided to halt the struggle, and our personnel were withdrawn.

As Che's wife, Aleida March, wrote in the foreword to his Congo diary: "Che, together with the group he led, aimed to strengthen as much as possible the liberation movement in the Congo, to achieve a united front, to select the best men and those prepared to continue the struggle for the fi nal liberation of Africa" (Guevara 2000:xlv). And according to Che's second in command in the Congo, Víctor Emilio Dreke, Che decided to participate in the Congo project after his African trip, even though this project went against his original idea of going to fi ght in Argentina (page xxiv).

I suppose Che decided to participate in the project after his African trip. It went against his original idea to go to fi ght in Argentina. The assassination of Lumumba and the general situation in the Congo led him to take an interest in the guerrilla struggle there. It enabled him to follow a double objective: to prepare a group for Latin America, and to create a third front [against imperialism], in Vietnam, Latin America, and Africa. These were the ideas he wished to bring to fruition. Africa seemed easier than Latin

America. . . . The moment had come to act in Africa.

M oreover, according to Pablo Rivalta, the Cuban ambassador in Tanzania who assisted Che's Congo mission, Che saw the Congo as a good site for a training base for liberation movements that would revolutionize all the African countries and in particular, bring down the infamous white supremacist regime in South Africa.

Despite the rumors at the time, Che's disagreement with Castro regarding Cuba's relationship with the Soviet Union was not the reason for his departure from Cuba, and this disagreement did not end the long-standing friendship between them. Nor did Cuba's relationship with the Soviet Union lead Castro to abandon his desire to see Cuba play an active role in the international struggle against U.S. and European imperialism. Castro was quite willing to send a contingent of Cubans, headed by Che, to assist the left-wing rebels in the Congo, who were then fi ghting against the pro-Western regime of Prime Minister Moise Tshombe.

The Congo became the scene of a bloody civil war following its independence from Belgium in 1960. The country's fi rst elected prime minister, Patrice Lumumba, was overthrown and then murdered by a U.S.-backed coup d'état in December 1960. When Tshombe, who was involved in Lumumba's assassination, subsequently became the country's head of state in 1964 with U.S. support, Lumumba's followers launched an armed uprising against him. In November 1964, with the intent of crushing this uprising, the U.S. government provided planes to transport Belgian troops and white mercenaries to the Congo.

B. ecause of the cold war confl ict at the time between the United States and its allies and the Soviet Union and its allies, the situation in the Congo became a major international political crisis. In December 1964, Fidel Castro sent Che to represent Cuba at the United Nations General Assembly in New York. In the well-publicized speech he gave at the General Assembly, Che denounced the involvement of the U.S. government and its allies in the Congo and other parts of Africa (Deutschmann 1997:286–88).

In this speech, Che reminded the members of the General Assembly that Lumumba was murdered following the occupation of the country by a United Nations force that Lumumba had requested. He said this force had allowed his opponents to capture and kill Lumumba with impunity. He claimed the United States and other Western imperialist countries used the United Nations to depose Lumumba and kill thousands of Congolese, and their purpose was to defend the superiority of the white race in Africa and to continue Western imperialist control over the Congo's vast mineral resources. And if this was not enough, he said, "the latest acts have fi lled the world with indignation" because they allowed one of Lumumba's murderers, Tshombe, to come to power illegally with the help of "Belgian paratroopers, carried by US planes, who took off from British bases" (Deutschmann:287).

Che went on to state: "Our free eyes open now on new horizons and can see what yesterday, in our condition as colonial slaves, we could not observe," namely, that so-called Western civilization uses "a showy façade" to disguise an ugly "picture of hyenas and jackals." He ended his comments on the Congo crisis by saying: "All free men of the world must be prepared to avenge the crime of the Congo." Only a few months later, in April 1965, Che led a secret contingent of 100 Cuban volunteers to assist the

Congolese rebels, who were fi ghting both the Tshombe regime and what they considered its Western imperialist backers.

T he idea of going to the Congo to assist the leftist rebels fi ghting the neocolonial regime there appealed to Che largely because of his fascination with the idea of linking the nations of Africa, Asia, and Latin America together in a common struggle against Western imperialism. And despite the lack of enthusiasm for the idea among many of the African leaders he met on his previous his trip to Africa, Che wanted to establish a Cuban-led military training center in the eastern Congo. He hoped revolutionaries from all over the African continent would come to this base to train and gain valuable fi ghting skills and experience that they would then take back to their respective countries (Anderson:623).

To prepare for the Congo expedition, Che removed himself from public view at the end of March 1965. By the end of April, his disappearance from public view had begun to cause a great deal of speculation both inside and outside Cuba about what had happened to him. On April 30, Fidel Castro was interviewed by a number of reporters, and in response to their questions about Che, he answered that he could say only that Che would always be where he could be of most use to the revolution. This statement, however, only served to intensify the speculation and rumors about Che's disappearance.

Che wrote a confi dential and rather personal letter of resignation to Castro when he left for the Congo. This letter (Gerassi 1968a:410–11), which Castro made public in October 1965, appears to have been designed among other purposes to absolve the Cuban government of all responsibility for Che's actions in the Congo in the event he was discovered, captured, or killed there.

Fidel:

I remember at this hour many things, when we met at Maria Antonia's house in Mexico, when you suggested that I come to Cuba, and the tension of the last minute preparations. One day they came around asking who to advise in case of death, and its real possibility struck us all. Afterward, we knew that it was certain, that in a revolution you die or triumph (if the revolution is a true one). Many of our comrades were left behind on the long road to victory. Today everything has a less dramatic tone because we are all more mature, but the same thing is repeating itself. I feel I have completed that part of my duty that has tied me to the Cuban revolution and so I say good-bye to you, our comrades, and to your people, who are now mine too.

I formally renounce my post in the directorate of the party, my post as minister, my rank of comandante, and my status as a Cuban. There is nothing legal that ties me to Cuba, only ties of another type that cannot be broken as in the case of offi ces. Making a summary of my past life, I think that I have worked with suffi cient honesty and dedication to consolidate the success of the revolution. My only fault of any gravity is that I did not confi de in you at the beginning in the Sierra Maestra and have not understood with suffi cient clarity your qualities as a leader and revolutionary.

I have lived magnifi cent days at your side and I have felt the pride of belonging to our people in the dark and bright days of the Caribbean crisis [Bay of Pigs invasion by U.S.-backed Cuban exiles]. Rarely has a statesman shone as brightly as you in those days. I feel proud of having followed you without hesitation, identifying myself with your way of thinking, seeing and appreciating both the dangers and principles. Other lands of the world now claim the assistance of my modest efforts. I can do what you now are prevented from doing because of your responsibility at the helm of Cuba, and so the time has come to separate. Let it be known that I do this both in pleasure and sorrow: here I leave the purest of my hopes as a builder and the most cherished of my loved ones and I leave a people who admitted me as one of their sons; this lacerates part of my spirit. To new fi elds of battle I will take the faith that you have given me, the revolutionary spirit of my people, and the feeling of carrying out the most sacred of duties: to fi ght against imperialism wherever it exists; this comforts and cures my pain abundantly.

O nce again I say that I free Cuba of all responsibility, except that which comes from her example. If my last hour should come under other skies, my last thought will be for the Cuban people and especially for you. I am grateful for your teaching and example, and I will be faithful to you until my last act. I have always identifi ed myself with the foreign policies of our revolution and will continue to do so. Wherever I go I will feel the responsibility of being a Cuban revolutionary, and I will act as one. I leave nothing material to my wife and children; and this doesn't bother me for I am happy that it is this way. I ask nothing for them, since the state will provide them enough to live and will educate them. There are many things I could tell you and our people, but I feel that this is not necessary. Words cannot express what I want to say, and it is not worth while to fi ll sheets of paper. Victory always! Country or death! My embrace with all revolutionary fervor.

Che

W hen Che left for the Congo in April 1965, he led a handpicked group of mostly black Cubans who had fought with him and Castro in the Sierra Maestra. Their clandestine mission was carefully planned by Cuban intelligence, which planted a false report in the Dominican Republic that Che had arrived in the capital of Santo Domingo in April and had been killed shortly thereafter in the civil war going on in that country at the time (Anderson 1997:638). Thus, while the CIA was looking for evidence of Che's presence in the Dominican Republic, he and his companions were able to leave Cuba, travel to Africa, and enter the Congo with complete secrecy.

C. he's reasons for leaving uba in 1965 to go fi ght in the Congo and later in 1966 to establish a guerrilla training base in Bolivia were twofold. He felt his mission in life was to carry out the struggle for the liberation of Latin America and the rest of the Third World from imperialist domination and capitalist exploitation. Moreover, he felt he would soon be too old to be able to physically carry out this kind of mission. Furthermore, to carry out this kind of mission, he needed the freedom of action that he could gain only if he was no longer a high-profi le offi cial in the Cuban government. His offi cial responsibilities required him to speak in the name of this government and to act in accordance with its policies and diplomatic relations (Taibo:530).

H e felt it was necessary to free himself from the constraints imposed on him by his offi cial obligations as an important leader in the Cuban government so that he could return to the life of a revolutionary guerrilla fi ghter and carry out the global struggle against Western imperialism, which he had come to consider his main mission in life. His total commitment to his convictions in this regard and the feeling that time was running out on his ability to fulfi ll his mission were his reasons for leaving Cuba in 1965.

A ccording to Fidel Castro, he knew Che had wanted to go to fi ght in South America for many years, since the time Che joined the Cuban revolutionary movement in Mexico. In fact, Che told Castro then that once the Cuban revolution triumphed he wanted to be free to go fi ght in Argentina. Castro revealed this in his 1987 interview with the Italian journalist Gianni Minà (Deutschmann 1994:116).

C he very much wanted to go to South America. This was an old idea of his, because when he joined us in Mexico . . . he did ask one thing: "The only thing I want after the victory of the revolution is to go fi ght in Argentina"—his country—"that you don't keep me from doing so, that no reasons of state will stand in the way." And I promised him that. It was a long way off, after all. Firstly, no one knew if we would win the war or who was going to be alive at the end—and he surely, because of his impetuousness, had little chance of coming out alive. . . . Once in a while, in the Sierra and afterward, he would remind me of this plan and promise. He was certainly farsighted in this.

A fter the success of the Cuban revolution, Castro said Che "grew more enthusiastic about the idea of making a revolution in South America," and as the years went by he became increasingly impatient to carry out his desire to play an important role in this historic struggle.

CHE'S AFRICAN DIARY

Che realized shortly after arriving in the Congo that the rebels could not win because of their corrupt and weak leaders, their failure to organize support among the local population, their distrust of one another, and their hopeless lack of discipline. In this regard, it is relevant to note the following observation he made in what has become known as his Congo diary (Guevara 2000:235):

T he leaders of the movement pass most of their time outside of the territory. . . . Organizational work is almost null, due to the fact that the mid-level leaders do not work, in fact they do not know how to work, and every one distrusts every one else. . . . Lack of discipline and lack of self-sacrifi ce are the dominant characteristics of the guerrilla troops. Naturally, with these troops one cannot win a war.

I n Tanzania after he was forced to leave the Congo, Che wrote a 153page manuscript about the failure of his Congo mission. Che wrote this account of his Congo experience during his stay in the Cuban embassy in Dar es Salaam, Tanzania, during the months he lived there in secrecy. This manuscript, *Pasajes de la guerra revolucionaria: Congo,* was kept secret for more than 30 years, until it was edited and fi rst published in 1999 by his wife Aleida March and Richard Gott (the English translation was published in 2000. See Guevara 2000).

T his ruthlessly honest document reveals among other things that Che decided he would accompany the contingent of armed Cubans sent to the Congo without fi rst informing and obtaining the consent of the Congolese rebel leaders such as Laurent Kabila. Thus, Che states in this document:

I hadn't told any of the Congolese about my decision to fi ght there. In my fi rst conversation with Kabila I had not been able to do so because nothing had yet been decided, and after the plan was approved [by Fidel Castro] it would have been dangerous for my project to be known before I arrived at my destination; there was a lot of hostile territory to cross. I decided, therefore, to present a fait accompli and act according to however they reacted to my presence. I was not unaware of the fact that a negative would place me in a diffi cult position, because now I couldn't go back, but I calculated that it would be diffi cult for them to refuse me. (page 10)

Although the Congolese rebel leaders did not object to Che's presence as the commander of the Cuban contingent, they were concerned about his presence in the Congo. Moreover, he found it diffi cult to meet with them and soon realized there was little prospect for the rebels to achieve victory since these leaders were ineffective and their forces were incapable of defeating the existing neocolonial regime, which had the backing of the Belgian, British, and U.S. governments.

C he also blamed himself for the failure of the Congo mission. He wrote: "I set off with more faith than ever in the guerrilla struggle, yet we failed. My responsibility is great; I shall not forget the defeat nor its most precious lessons. I learned certain things in the Congo. Some mistakes I will never make again, others perhaps I will—and there will be new ones that I shall commit" (Guevara 2000:235).

A lthough he said he continued to have faith in his foco theory for creating a popular revolution, he made the following scathing critique of his own actions in the Congo:

I was at the head of a group of Cubans, no more than one company strong, and my function was to be their real leader who carried them to the victory that would hasten the development of a genuine popular army. My peculiar situation, however, made of me a soldier representing a foreign power, an instructor of Cubans and Congolese, a strategist, and a high fl ying politician in an unfamiliar setting. . . . Had I been a more authentic soldier, I might have had more infl uence in the other spheres of my complicated relationships. I have described how I reached the point of safeguarding the cadre (my own precious person) at particularly disastrous moments in which I found myself, and how I allowed subjective considerations to gain the upper hand in the closing moments.

F rom this passage in his diary, it is clear that Che was deeply critical of his own behavior and the many limitations he confronted in the Congo. He engaged in this self-critique with a view to avoiding repetition in the future of the errors that he felt he had committed in the Congo.

However, Che's subsequent mission to Bolivia appears to have failed for some of the same reasons as the Congo mission. For example, in Bolivia Che repeated the tactic of inserting himself secretly into another country at the head of a foreign military group and into a situation that lacked both the objective and subjective conditions necessary for a successful revolutionary movement.

THE LEGACY OF CHE'S MISSION IN AFRICA

I t is interesting to note that although Che's mission to the Congo was a bitter defeat for him and his Cuban companions, the lessons Cuba's leaders learned from this unsuccessful effort to assist the Congolese rebels helped them to be much more successful in the military and political support they provided to liberation movements and leftist governments throughout Africa during the following decades. Without a doubt, the best example of this success was Cuba's involvement in Angola.

B etween April 1965, when Che fi rst promised Antônio Agostinho Neto the leader of the liberation movement fi ghting the Portuguese colonial rulers of Angola that Cuba would assist the liberation struggle in his country, and May 1991, when the last Cuban combatants left Angola, some 450,000 Cubans (7% of the Cuban population) had served in this worn-torn country (Harris 2009). They helped the liberation movement gain Angola's independence and then helped the new government of President Neto defeat two South African military interventions and a bloody insurgency backed by the U.S. government. They also helped the Angolan government repulse an invasion from Zaire (now the Democratic Republic of the Congo) in the longest and largest military campaign in Africa since World War II.

Cuban support played a key role in Angola's liberation and defense and in the liberation of Guinea-Bissau and Cape Verde from Portuguese colonial domination, and Cuba also helped defend the newly independent government of the Congo Republic (Brazzaville), formerly a French colony, from neocolonial forces intent on overturning it. They played an important role in the liberation of Mozambique from Portuguese colonial rule, as well as the liberation of the white-settler-controlled former British colony of Rhodesia (Zimbabwe). Moreover, the Cuban military victories against the white South African forces in Angola greatly contributed to the liberation of Namibia and to the ultimate downfall of the white supremacist apartheid regime in South Africa itself. This regime was greatly weakened by the demoralizing defeat the combined Cuban, Angolan, and Namibian forces infl icted on the white South African troops in Angola and Namibia.

Nelson Mandela, the fi rst president of the new Republic of South Africa, established after the downfall of the racist apartheid regime in that country, is among the many African leaders who have praised the Cubans for the assistance they provided in these struggles for independence. He has repeatedly thanked the Cubans for their contribution to the victory of his people over racist domination and imperialism. For example, at the public opening of the Southern Africa–Cuba Solidarity Conference in 1995, President Mandela (1995) said:

Cubans came to our region as doctors, teachers, soldiers, agricultural experts, but never as colonizers. They have shared the same trenches with us in the struggle against colonialism, underdevelopment, and apartheid. Hundreds of Cubans have given their lives, literally, in a struggle that was, fi rst and foremost, not theirs but ours. As Southern Africans we salute them. We vow never to forget this unparalleled example of selfl ess internationalism.

At a more individual level, Che's brief presence in the Congo changed dramatically the life of the Congolese teenager who served as his translator during the months he and his companions operated in the Fizi Baraka mountain range near the border between the Congo and Tanzania. Freddy Ilanga, who spoke both Swahili and French, had been a newspaper vendor and was just 16 years old when he was assigned by the rebel leadership to serve as Che's translator during the time he and his Cuban comrades carried out their then secret mission of providing support to the Congolese rebels. Freddy Ilanga's brief encounter with the legendary Che and his Cuban companions placed him on the path of an incredible journey that took him from being a teenage rebel in the eastern Congo to Cuba where he studied medicine, married a Cuban woman, and became a brain surgeon.

As a young African who saw the whites in his country as racist oppressors, he knew nothing about the Cuban Revolution and at fi rst he considered Che to be a sarcastic white man (Doyle 2004). But he soon came to admire Che. He was particularly impressed with how Che treated the Africans around him with respect. In those days in the Congo, this was something Freddy had never seen.

S hortly before Che and his companions pulled out of the Congo, they arranged for Freddy to be sent to Cuba, where he fi nished his schooling, went to the university to become a doctor, and then specialized in pediatric neurosurgery. Although Freddy never returned to the Congo before he died in Cuba, today in Africa there are hundreds of Cuban doctors and African doctors who were trained in Cuba (Harris 2009).

Ironically, Kabila seized control of the government of the Congo in 1997, at the head of a military force that originated in the same region of the country where Che and his Cuban comrades had established their training base in 1965. Backed by the governments of Rwanda and Uganda, Kabila's forces managed to topple the long-time dictatorial regime of General Mobutu Sese Seko, the U.S.-backed military strongman who had seized power in November 1965, the same month Che and his men were forced to abandon their mission in the Congo. Kabila was assassinated by a member of his own staff in an unsuccessful coup attempt in 2001, and his son replaced him as the Congolese head of state.

CHE'S SECRET RETURN TO CUBA IN 1966

In November 1965, Che left the Congo as secretly as he had entered seven months earlier. After leaving the Congo, he spent a couple of months in secrecy in the Cuban embassy in Dar es Salaam, Tanzania. During this time, Castro gave Che's wife, Aleida, permission to visit him, and she arrived in Tanzania in mid-January 1966 (March 2008:200). For Aleida, this visit was what she had dreamed might happen some day. It enabled them to be completely alone together without their children and the constant circle of subordinates and comrades that had previously surrounded him in Cuba.

During their stay in the Cuban embassy in Dar es Salaam, they slept, ate, read, and conversed in a large dining room that was converted into living quarters for them. During this time, Che went over the notes he had written during his seven months in the Congo and wrote a lengthy manuscript that was primarily intended as a report for Cuba's top leaders on the failure of his mission and what he had learned about the possibilities for assisting liberation movements and leftist governments in Africa.

This manuscript was read by Fidel Castro and a few other key offi cials of the Cuban government but kept secret for more than 30 years . As in the case of his Bolivian diary, Aleida March played a central role in its publication. It was published in English with the title *The African Dream: The Diaries of the Revolutionary War in the Congo*, with the addition of an introduction written by the well-known British journalist and historian Richard Gott (2000).

I n Castro's 1987 interview with the Italian journalist mentioned above, he revealed what happened after Che was forced to withdraw from the Congo (Deutschmann 1994:119). According to Castro:

Having now spent about six months in Zaire, Che stayed for a while in Tanzania, assessing the experience he had just lived through. His conduct on the mission was, as always, exemplary to the highest degree. His stay in Africa was temporary, awaiting the creation of conditions for traveling to South America.

But as Castro explained in this interview, Che's situation was now greatly complicated by the fact that during his absence his resignation letter had been made public by the Cuban government in response to the growing rumors and outrageous stories circulating about his mysterious disappearance from public view in Cuba. To quote Castro (pages 119–20):

O nce the letter had been made public—politically it had become unavoidable to publish it—Che, with his particular character, felt very awkward about returning to Cuba after having said farewell.

But in the end, I persuaded him to return, because it was the best move given all the practical matters he wanted to take care of. So, he secretly returned to Cuba. He stayed several months, training in a remote mountain region . . . with those who were to accompany him [to Bolivia].

I t was a bitter blow for him to return secretly to Cuba after spending seven months in the Congo without having anything to show for his efforts and after having resigned his important positions in the Cuban government. The experience, however, seems to have made Che more determined than ever to undertake a successful revolutionary mission outside of Cuba, but this time in his native South America.

U pon his return to Cuba from the Congo, Che found solace in the fact that one of his grandest dreams had come true; an intercontinental organization representing the underdeveloped countries of the world, with its headquarters in Cuba, had been founded only a few months before his return by Fidel Castro. From January 3 to 15, 1966, the fi rst conference of the Organization of Solidarity of Asian, African, and Latin American Peoples—referred to thereafter as the Tricontinental—was held in Havana, with some 400 delegates from the underdeveloped world attending. As it turned out, Che's revolutionary ideas were the central topic of discussion among the delegates, and this undoubtedly reinforced his determination to carry out the realization of one of his oldest dreams: the liberation of Latin America's oppressed and exploited masses. This dream was bolstered by his belief that Cuba would become truly independent of the Soviet Union only when additional revolutionary governments were established in Latin America that could provide support to Cuba.

C he's return to Cuba was never made public (Deutschmann 1994:119). He remained in hiding during the entire period that he stayed there. Almost immediately after his return, he began to prepare a new mission that he felt would not have the limitations of the abortive undertaking in the Congo. He chose Bolivia as the site for a revolutionary guerrilla foco, which he himself would organize and lead. In October 1966, he once again left Cuba, as secretly as he had entered, to begin this undertaking.

CHAPTER THREE

Che's Final Mission in Bolivia

Che's fi nal mission was carried out in Bolivia, in the heart of South America. Bolivia is a starkly beautiful country that combines towering snow-capped mountains and a high-altitude, windswept, treeless dry plateau with deep tropical valleys and a wide expanse of tropical lowlands in the eastern portion of the country that borders Brazil. The country is divided into two distinctive parts by the massive wall of the Andes Mountains, which traverse the country from north to south. The mountains and high plateau in the western portion of the country have such an otherworldly terrain and such unusual colors that they look more like Nepal or the alternate reality of another planet than a country in the heart of the South American continent near the equator. This part of the country contains the *altiplano,* the great high plateau of the South American continent. Here the descendants of the ancient Incan civilization, with their herds of llamas, live an impoverished existence some two and a half miles above sea level. The vastness and barrenness of this windy plateau give it a haunting beauty all its own, and anyone who has been to this part of the world carries away unforgettable memories of magnifi cent panoramas, azure blue skies fi lled with white puffy clouds that look close enough to touch, and snow-covered peaks bathed in the soft, multicolored glow of an indescribably beautiful sunset.

O n the altiplano are Bolivia's major mining centers and the focal point of national politics, the capital city of La Paz. Situated at 11,900 feet in a deep basin on the altiplano, La Paz is the highest capital city in the world. The approach by land to the city is from the altiplano. Consequently, the fi rst view one receives of La Paz is from some 2,000 feet directly above it. The view of the shiny tin-roofed city in the basin below takes one's breath away. Far below sprawls the glittering city and, in the distance beyond, the snowy peaks of the mystical Mount Illimani (sacred to the Incas) tower to a height of over 21,000 feet.

L a Paz is a fascinating blend of the old and new. Together with modern buildings and late-model cars, one sees churches built by the Spaniards over four centuries ago; and in every street, Indian women with their characteristic bowler hats, colorful shawls, and babies carried on their backs. It is a bustling, sunny city, fi lled with color, lots of hilly streets, Spanish colonial style buildings, and an atmosphere of excitement and activity. It has a breezy, cool, and dry climate, and because it is so high the atmosphere is thin and it is easy to lose one's breath without too much exertion.

O ver the mountains from La Paz lies the city of Cochabamba, an important agricultural center in the heart of an 8,400-foot-high valley where the climate is temperate and the soil quite fertile. Farther east, the mountains drop toward the tropical savannas and plains of eastern Bolivia. The most important city in this area is Santa Cruz, located at the foot of the eastern slopes of the Andes. Santa Cruz is known for its colonial Spanish architecture and its beautiful women of Spanish descent, but today it has all the characteristics of a boom city. The growing economy of the area is based on sugar, cotton, rice, oil, and cocaine (it was rumored in the 1980s and 1990s to be the capital of Bolivia's international cocaine trade). Approximately 200 miles south of Santa Cruz lies the town of Camiri, the only other sizable urban center in the eastern part of the country. Camiri is Bolivia's oil and gas center, and although it is not comparable to Santa Cruz in either importance or size, it too has experienced an economic boom.

D espite the eastern portion of Bolivia accounting for approximately 70 percent of the total land area of the country, only about one-fourth of Bolivia's small population lives east of the Andes (the population of Bolivia was approximately 4 million in 1967 when Che and his guerrilla force were there and today it is over 9 million). The real heartland of Bolivia is located on the *altiplano*. It is there the vast majority of the country's population live and there the main loci of economic and political power are to be found. Moreover, most of the important events in Bolivian political history have taken place on the altiplano.

B efore choosing Bolivia as the site of his guerrilla operation, Che considered several other countries, particularly Argentina and Peru. There was nothing he would have liked better than to bring the revolution to his native Argentina. This was something he had planned for many years. But it was obvious the situation in Argentina was not favorable for such an undertaking in 1966. In 1964, a Cuban-backed and Guevara-inspired guerrilla force attempted to establish itself in northern Argentina, but the effort ended in total failure a few months later without having realized a single military engagement (Castañeda

1997: 247–50). The leader of this group was the Argentine Jorge Masetti, who was a close friend of Che's in Cuba. Together they had planned the Argentine operation in early 1963. Their objective at the time was to establish a chain of guerrilla focos from northern Argentina to Peru.

H owever, Masetti's small force was defeated by the harsh environment of northern Argentina, where his group tried to establish a guerrilla foco, their poor organization, and their inability to attract any popular support. In the end, those members of his guerrilla band who did not die from starvation and exposure were either taken prisoner or killed by the Argentine police and armed forces. The death of Masetti and the three Cuban comrades from Guevara's own bodyguard who had gone with Masetti to help establish the guerrilla foco in Argentina was a bitter reminder to Che that Argentina was not the most suitable place for him to establish an armed revolutionary movement in 1966.

A s for Peru, the situation there was not any more favorable than in Argentina. In 1966 that country had an elected civilian government with a moderately progressive program (Taibo 1996:612–16). Moreover, the government and the army had effectively suppressed several guerrilla uprisings in isolated parts of the country during the preceding two years. Che also considered Colombia, Venezuela, and Brazil, but never very seriously (Anderson 1997:678). In the end, Bolivia was chosen because it was considered to have the best revolutionary potential and because it afforded the ideal strategic location. It was in the center of the continent and bordered Argentina, Brazil, Chile, Paraguay, and Peru.

C he had been in Bolivia for a short time in 1953, when he had traveled there with his friend Carlos "Calica" Ferrer, and his impression of the country at that time undoubtedly infl uenced his choice of Bolivia in 1966. As previously mentioned in chapter 3, he was there during a period when the country was literally infected with revolutionary enthusiasm. Less than a year before, thousands of miners, peasants, and deserters from the Bolivian army had revolted and brought down the then existing military regime. When Che arrived in La Paz in 1953, the old army had been disbanded, the largest foreign-owned mines in the country had been nationalized, and the peasants had taken possession of many of the large landed estates following the enactment of the new government's agrarian reform law. The streets were fi lled with singing and loud demonstrations, and everywhere he saw the armed peasants and workers of the revolutionary militia. He surely must have thought of these armed peasants and workers in 1966 when he chose Bolivia as the place to initiate his revolutionary movement, since he fi rmly believed the revolution of those days had been subsequently betrayed by opportunistic politicians and army generals corrupted by *Yanqui* dollars, U.S. military advisers, and the CIA.

M ost of Che's information on Bolivia appears to have come from several Bolivian Communists, who had helped previously with the Masetti operation, and from Che's aide, José María Martínez Tamayo (Papi) who was sent to Bolivia in March 1966 to make the preliminary preparations for Che's new operation (Castañeda 1997:334). Most of these Bolivian Communists had received military training in Cuba. They assured Papi the country was ripe for a Cuban-type revolution and all that was needed was Cuban support. They informed him there was widespread discontent in Bolivia with the military-backed regime of President

Barrientos, and they contended this government could fall at any moment. They also spoke of the country's strong revolutionary tradition, of the visible and often resented U.S.-dominant presence in the country's economic and political affairs, and of how the mining centers were virtual caldrons of rebellion. Finally, they confi rmed what Che and the Cuban intelligence service already knew, that the Bolivian security and military forces were perhaps the most ineffective and badly organized in Latin America.

As a result, Che decided Bolivia was the appropriate location for his operation. He minimized the fact that Bolivia's Communists were badly split along pro-Soviet and pro-Chinese lines and the leader of Bolivia's pro-Soviet Communist Party, Mario Monje, had told Castro during the Tricontinental conference in 1966 he was interested himself in establishing a guerrilla foco in Bolivia.

Bolivia had great strategic importance for Che since it is the *corazón* (heart) of South America and borders most of the major countries on the continent. From Bolivia, Che hoped his revolutionary effort would extend in every direction and involve all of South America. The expedition to Bolivia was designed to create a guerrilla *madre,* or mother base, that would provide training and a jumping-off point for a series of

revolutionary guerrilla forces that would engulf the entire continent in a revolutionary struggle for a unifi ed and socialist Latin America (Siles del Valle 1996:29–38).

O nce he had decided on Bolivia, Che selected the southeast of the country for his initial guerrilla foco. He chose the southeast because it offered relatively close access to neighboring Argentina, Brazil, Chile, and Paraguay. In addition, he assumed that in this area, because of its isolation and sparse population, his guerrilla force would be able to develop without being discovered before it was ready to begin operations. This region of the country is part of the Gran Chaco region, which stretches into Paraguay. Its climate is semiarid to semi-tropical and has only two seasons: summer and winter. There are rain and hot, humid conditions during the summer months from December through March, but the winter months from April through November consist of dry, hot days and cool nights, when the temperature can drop below freezing. Median temperatures vary from 73 to 83 degrees F (23 to 28 degrees C), but this region can have the hottest days in Bolivia. When the humidity is low the dry heat can reach extreme temperatures, up to 115 degrees F (46 degrees C) during the daytime.

The specific location chosen as the central base of operations for Che's group was the Ñancahuazú River valley. In this semi-tropical, scrubforested valley, Che planned to train the nucleus of his guerrilla movement, build fortifi cations, and establish caches of supplies and arms. Once his force was ready for combat, he planned to move north and threaten three of Bolivia's major cities: Cochabamba, Santa Cruz, and Sucre. This would enable the guerrillas to control the railway line that runs from northern Argentina to Santa Cruz, as well as to cut the U.S.-owned Gulf Oil Company pipeline that ran from Santa Cruz to Camiri. Later, Che planned to locate a second guerrilla base farther east, on the slopes of the Andes.

Che planned to begin military operations in May 1967, following six months of preparation. In the opening phase, he planned to divide his force into several small bands and have them strike simultaneously at widely dispersed points north of the Ñancahuazú area. In this way he hoped to force the Bolivian army to disperse its forces over a large area, while his guerrillas made a slow withdrawal toward the Ñancahuazú River valley, where they could rely on previously established caches of supplies and fortifi cations. Che reasoned that if the inexperienced Bolivian army attempted to follow the guerrillas into the Ñancahuazú River valley, they would be at the mercy of these guerrilla bands. As his guerrillas demonstrated their capacity to win victories against the Bolivian army, Che believed many of the country's peasants and miners would come to the support of the movement.

C he also assumed that once his guerrilla movement was well established and drawing widespread support and public attention, conditions would become more favorable for guerrilla operations in Peru and Argentina (Taibo 1996:615). He planned to have a guerrilla group operating in the Ayacucho region of Peru by the end of 1967 and another force in northern Argentina sometime after that. The Bolivian base of operations was to be a training ground for the nucleus of both the Peruvian and Argentine forces.

Che revealed his overall strategy in the message he sent to the second conference of the Tricontinental in 1967. It was entitled: "Create Two, Three, Many Vietnams." In this message, it is clear he believed a successful guerrilla insurgency in Latin America would force the United States to commit itself directly to the contest, creating a second Vietnam in the heart of South America. His conception of the course of events that would follow the appearance of his guerrilla movement in Bolivia is revealed in the following passage from his message to the conference:

New outbreaks of war will appear in these and other Latin American countries, as has already occurred in Bolivia. And they will continue to grow, with all the vicissitudes involved in this dangerous occupation of the modern revolutionist. Many will die, victims of their own errors; others will fall in the diffi cult combat to come; new fi ghters and new leaders will arise in the heat of the revolutionary struggle. . . . The Yankee agents of repression will increase in number. Today there are advisers in all countries where armed struggle is going on. . . . Little by little the obsolete weapons that are suffi cient for the suppression of small armed bands will be converted by the Americans into modern arms, and American advisers will be converted into combatants, until, in a given moment, they will see themselves obligated to send increasing quantities of regular troops to assure the relative stability of a power whose puppet national army disintegrates before the attacks of the guerrillas. This is the road of Vietnam. It is the road that other people will follow, and it is the road that Latin America will follow. . . . We must defi nitely keep in mind that imperialism is a world system, the fi nal stage of capitalism, and that it must be beaten in a great worldwide confrontation. (Deutschmann 1997:322–23)

From this message, it is clear Che was counting on U.S involvement in Bolivia and he saw this as a means of gaining the support of both Bolivian and international public opinion.

A s for the ultimate goal of the continental revolutionary movement Che was hoping to start in Bolivia, this too was revealed in his message to the Tricontinental conference. He said:

W e can summarize our hopes for victory as follows: the destruction of imperialism through the elimination of its strongest bulwark: the imperial dominion of the United States of North America. This will be accomplished through the gradual liberation of its subject peoples, either one by one or by groups, drawing the enemy into a diffi cult struggle outside of its territory; and cutting it off from its bases of support, i.e., its dependent territories.

Thus, for Che, Bolivia was to be the fi rst step in a grand plan to liberate all of Latin America from U.S. infl uence and convert it into a bastion of socialism and anti-imperialism. Everything, therefore, depended on successfully establishing in Bolivia a guerrilla madre that would develop into a successful revolutionary movement of continental dimensions.

Prophetically, however, the fi nal sentences in his message to the Tricontinental Conference suggested what was to come:

Wherever death may surprise us, let it be welcome if our battle cry has reached even one receptive ear; if another hand reaches out to take up our arms, and other men come forward to join in our funeral dirge with the rattling of machine guns and with new cries of battle and victory.

Death did surprise Che in Bolivia, and his battle cry has reached many receptive ears over the years since then.

C he could not seek the support of the pro-Chinese Communists in Bolivia because the leaders of the rival pro-Soviet Communists in Bolivia had told Fidel Castro their party planned to set up a guerrilla foco in the country. It appears these leaders purposely misled Castro into believing they were going to do this in order to outfl ank the more militant, proChinese Communists, who they were afraid were interested in doing this with Cuban help (Anderson:682–87). Che was aware of this political situation, and he distrusted Monje and the other leaders of Bolivia's proSoviet Communist Party. Consequently, he relied primarily on a small number of pro-Cuba supporters within Monje's pro-Soviet Communist party to make the preliminary preparations for his guerrilla operation. These were individuals who had previously spent some time training in Cuba, and Che knew many of them personally. He felt they could be trusted to lay the groundwork for his operation without telling even the leadership of their party what they were doing.

The most important of Che's Bolivian contacts were two brothers— Roberto "Coco" and Guido "Inti" Peredo. These two brothers helped convince Che that Bolivia was the ideal base for a guerrilla operation. Because of this and perhaps because Che saw these two brothers as the future Raúl and Fidel Castro of Bolivia, he entrusted them with the most important aspects of the preliminary preparations for his guerrilla foco.

C oco and Inti had participated in the efforts that were made in 1960 to establish guerrilla focos in Salta, Argentina, and Puerto Maldonado, Peru. They had joined the Communist Party's youth wing at an early age and their previous efforts to establish Cuban-style guerrilla focos made them ideal candidates for the guerrilla force Che organized in Bolivia. They also owned and operated a taxi in La Paz. This vocation gave them a perfect cover for their clandestine activities. Sometime during the summer of 1966, they both traveled to the southeast and located themselves in Camiri, Bolivia's petroleum center. There they made friends with some of the local inhabitants and let it be known they were interested in buying land in the area north of Camiri for the purpose of establishing a ranch and cereal farm.

In September they succeeded in buying an abandoned ranch in a largely uninhabited region near the Ñancahuazú River, 50 miles north of Camiri. In addition, they rented some adjacent property from their only neighbor, Ciro

Argañaraz, a local landowner and cattle rancher.

While Inti returned to La Paz to take care of their personal affairs, Coco began readying the ranch for the arrival of Che and his Cuban comrades. He contracted two local men to work the ranch and planted several different varieties of cereals. He also bought some cattle, hogs, and poultry. During this period, Coco traveled the winding dirt road from the ranch to Camiri in his new Toyota jeep almost daily. On this road, about 12 miles from the ranch, is the small village of Lagunillas. Coco stopped there on several occasions to buy vegetables and fruit. The large amounts of supplies he transported to the ranch in his jeep aroused the suspicion of many of the local villagers. Many of them, as well as the landowner, Argañaraz, assumed the Peredo brothers were cocaine merchants or cattle thieves.

M eanwhile, in La Paz, Che's other Bolivian collaborators made arrangements for receiving Che's group and their equipment. They obtained a house and a warehouse in the center of the city, where they stored arms and ammunition, which they received hidden in bags of cement mix. These were shipped from Cuba to the port of Arica in northern Chile and from there sent by rail to La Paz.

One of Che's prime contacts in La Paz during this period, and later the only female member of his guerrilla force, was a woman known by the code name of Tania. Her real name was Haydée Tamara Bunke. She was a German Argentine Che had met in Communist East Germany and who had come to Cuba on the invitation of Che. While there, she became a member of the small circle of Argentines who met frequently at Che's house. Tania left Cuba and entered Bolivia in 1964 with a false Argentine passport. In early 1965 she obtained a job working for

Gonzalo López, director of information in the presidential palace. In addition to working for López, Tania also successfully passed herself off as a professor of languages. This gave her an opportunity to travel widely throughout the country, ostensibly for the purpose of studying the languages and folk songs of the indigenous (Indian) population. In her spare time she worked her way into some of the capital's artistic, cultural, and diplomatic circles. Her contacts provided Che with valuable information and assistance. Through her direct access to documents and forms in the Information Offi ce of the Presidency she was later able to provide Che and some of his Cuban companions with very impressive credentials that allowed them to travel quite freely within the country.

C he arrived in Bolivia, around November 1, 1966, on a plane from São Paolo, Brazil. He entered Bolivia as a clean-shaven, bald man wearing glasses. He had two false Uruguayan passports, and it is not clear which of the two he actually used to enter Bolivia. The passports were issued under the names of Ramón Benitez and Adolfo Mena. The fi ngerprints on both passports are exactly the same as those that were later identifi ed by various governments as belonging to Che. The photographs on both passports are also the same. On close examination they reveal a clean-shaven, bald Che Guevara wearing glasses. Both passports have the same dates of entry and departure from Madrid airport.

Che was accompanied by one of his longtime Cuban comrades: Alberto Fernández (whose code name was Pacho). Upon arrival they contacted Tania, and she gave Che a truly extraordinary document: it accredited Che (Adolfo Mena in this case) as a special envoy of the Organization of American States. According to this document, he was in Bolivia to conduct research on the social and economic relations prevailing in the rural areas of Bolivia.

With Che carrying this document, Che and Pacho traveled to the Ñancahuazú ranch in two separate jeeps, arriving there the night of November 6. Che brought to Bolivia a contingent of 12 Cubans. Most of the members of this handpicked group were veterans of Che's guerrilla column in the Sierra Maestra. Some held the rank of comandante in the Cuban army. Many of them had served in important posts in the Cuban government and armed forces, and several were members of the Central Committee of the Cuban Communist Party. All of these individuals were tied to Che by unquestioning personal loyalty. Some had been with him in the Congo. They were willing to follow him to hell if he asked them to do so, and in the end only three of them returned home to Cuba alive.

T he Bolivian members of the guerrilla force were largely recruited by Coco and two other Bolivian agents, known by the code names of Rodolfo and Sánchez. The latter two men also served as liaisons between Che's group and the support network in the urban areas during the period before Che's guerrilla force was discovered. The entry in Che's diary at the end of November 1966 reveals he hoped to increase the number of Bolivians in his force to at least 20 before beginning military operations.

I n December at the Ñancahuazú ranch he met with Mario Monje, the leader of the pro-Soviet Bolivian Communist Party, to discuss the possibility of receiving men and assistance from his party. However, Monje refused to support the guerrilla operation and send men unless he was in charge of it. He made it clear his party could not offi cially support the guerrilla operation. However, he offered to resign from the party, obtain at least its neutrality, and bring several cadres of men to join those already in training, provided Che agreed to give him both the political and military command of the entire operation and a free hand to seek the support of the Communist parties in the other South American countries where Che planned to extend his guerrilla movement.

M onje's conditions for supporting the guerrilla movement were totally unacceptable to Che. He told Monje he could accept no conditions concerning his leadership of the military operations. He knew, in the kind of revolutionary struggle he was planning, the military leadership of the struggle would have to come from the guerrilla force itself, not from a politician or group of politicians hundreds of miles from the scene of battle. Nor was he about to turn over the command of a movement that, in its fi nal phase, would engulf all of Latin America to someone he considered lacked both the proper revolutionary vision as well as the necessary military experience. As for Monje's resigning from his position as leader of the party, Che said he considered this a tremendous error, since it would accommodate those in his party who should be publicly condemned for their hypocrisy.

Che's experience in the Congo also led him to reject Monje's conditions. The poor leadership of the Congolese rebels provided by their leaders such as Laurent Kabila was certainly on his mind and his experience in the Congo made him all the more determined to keep control over both the political and military direction of the guerrilla force in Bolivia rather than relinquish it to weak and untrustworthy local political leaders such as Monje (Guevara 2000:x–xi).

Monje met with the Bolivians in Che's group and told them they could stay with Che and be expelled from the party, or they could support the party and return with him to La Paz. Much to Monje's surprise, all the Bolivians present said they preferred to stay with Che. The next morning, Monje announced he was leaving for La Paz. Che realized Monje had disagreed with him over who should command the movement as a pretext to escape any responsibility for cooperating with Che's group. Che appears to have seen through Monje's subterfuge at the time; he noted in his diary that Monje had discovered from Coco that he (Che) would not compromise on the crucial question of who was to lead the movement. Che realized Monje had disagreed with him over who should command the movement so that he would have an excuse to not support Che's group.

If Monje had accepted the political leadership of the movement (while deferring to Che's military leadership) and had sent members of his party to fi ght with Che's nuclear group, then the guerrilla operation might not have suffered later from the stigma of being directed and organized by foreigners. After Che's guerrilla force was discovered and it became known it was led by Che and a group of Cubans, the Bolivian government was able to argue convincingly that the guerrillas were foreigners intervening in the domestic affairs of the country.

By the end of March 1967, Che had succeeded in recruiting approximately 20 Bolivians. Some had trained like Coco and Inti in Cuba specifi cally for fi ghting in the guerrilla operation. The remainder were dissident members of the youth wing of Monje's party and unemployed miners from the tin-mining areas on Bolivia's high plateau.

T he unemployed miners were recruited by Moisés Guevara (no relation to Che), an important union leader among the leftist tin miners in Oruro. Moisés had broken away from the pro-Chinese Communist Party in Bolivia and had traveled several times to Cuba, where he had met Che. Although Monje was opposed to involving Moisés in the guerrilla force, Che's Bolivian contacts invited Moisés to join the force with some of his miners. Moisés agreed and brought eight men with him to the Ñancahuazú camp in February 1967.

In addition to the Cubans and the Bolivians, Che's guerrilla force included among its members three Peruvians known by the code names of El Chino, Negro, and Eustaquio, respectively. El Chino (Juan Pablo Chang, who was a Peruvian of Chinese descent) was supposed to establish Che's planned guerrilla foco in Peru. He brought Eustaquio, a radio operator, and Negro, a physician, to Che's camp during the latter part of February. They were to be joined later by an additional number of Peruvians who were to train with Che's force and then return to their country to start another guerrilla foco there.

T he total number of combatants in the guerrilla force stood at 39 when the fi rst encounter between the army and Che's group took place on March 23, 1967. Most of the leadership positions were held by Cubans. Che appointed his old comrade in arms from the Sierra Maestra Comandante Juan Vitalio Acuña (code name Joaquín) as his second in command of the guerrilla force and also leader of the rearguard. He also appointed Cubans to the posts of leader of the vanguard, chief of operations, chief of services, and chief of supplies. Inti and Coco were the only two Bolivians entrusted with any leadership responsibilities. Inti was placed in charge of fi nances and appointed political commissar to the Bolivians. Coco, who was initially placed in charge of urban contacts and recruitment, was later incorporated into the guerrilla force and assigned various responsibilities.

N o additions to the guerrilla force took place after the outbreak of hostilities in late March. Instead, the size of Che's force was steadily reduced as each encounter with the army took its toll. Che had hoped to recruit peasants from the local area once his force began operations, but he failed to recruit even a single peasant after the fi ghting began.

C he's original plan was to begin military operations north of the Rio Grande and then slowly withdraw southward across a terrain carefully prepared with caches of arms and ammunition, food supplies, and fortifi ed bases. He needed perhaps another month before this plan would have been ready to be put into operation. But he had to discard it when the army discovered his main base after receiving credible reports about the presence of guerrillas in the Ñancahuazú area during the fi rst few weeks of March.

O n the morning of March 11, two of Moisés Guevara's new recruits left the main camp, ostensibly to go hunting. They took the path leading down to the river, but instead of going to the east, where the best hunting area was, they disappeared in the direction of Camiri. A few days later, they were arrested and brought to the headquarters of the Fourth Army Division in Camiri. There they gave their captors a detailed report concerning all they knew about the guerrilla operation. They gave the army detailed information about the location of the guerrillas' camp, the number of people there, and most of the guerrilla force being away at the time on a training and reconnaissance march to the north. They said they had been told Che Guevara was the leader of the operation and he was with the others in the north.

T he information these two deserters and several local people gave the Bolivian authorities led to the discovery and subsequent annihilation of Che's guerrilla force. This information enabled the army to locate Che's main base before he and his men were ready to begin military operations. It also gave the army the initiative from the beginning of the confl ict until its tragic termination some six months later. Timing was a crucial factor in Che's strategy, and the premature initiation of hostilities threw his whole operation off balance. His small force of men was never really able to recover from the shock of having their central base discovered before they were ready to begin fi ghting. All of Che's subsequent efforts were little more than futile, though valiant, attempts to put up a good fi ght in the face of overwhelming odds. He and his men seem to have deluded themselves during the fi rst few months of fi ghting into believing their operation still could succeed, but in reality their fate was sealed from the beginning. It was just a matter of time before they were caught or killed.

C he had written of the extreme danger a guerrilla force faces during its preparatory stage in "Guerrilla Warfare: A Method." He pointed out that the future of a revolutionary movement depends on how the nuclear guerrilla force handles itself when the enemy fi rst moves against it. According to Che, unless the guerrillas are able to develop their

capacity to attack the enemy during the early stage of the struggle, they have little prospect of surviving (in Guevara 1963).

A s a result of the army's discovery of their main base, Che and his men were forced to withdraw into a relatively confi ned area. He had originally planned to have his force operate across a zone carefully prepared with caches of supplies and fortifi ed bases, but the army's discovery of their main base forced Che and his men to move into an area about which they knew very little and where they had diffi culty fi nding food and places to hide.

Only Che's will to succeed and his refusal to accept defeat can explain his optimism about the future of his guerrilla operation after the discovery of his force at the end of March. Anyone else undoubtedly would have concluded under the circumstances there was no choice but to abandon the entire venture and escape while it was still possible to do so. But not Che; until the end he continued to believe his effort would succeed. Perhaps he kept thinking of how high the odds had been against the success of Castro's operation after the *Granma* disaster, when only 12 members of the original 80-man invasion force survived the landing on Cuban soil and made their way to the Sierra Maestra.

CHAPTER FOUR

The Tragic Death of a Revolutionary

Between March 23, 1967, when Che's guerrilla force was fi rst discovered by the Bolivian authorities and October 8 when Che was captured, his small guerrilla force was able to carry out a series of hit and run attacks on the Bolivian army. (The information in this chapter relies heavily upon the author's original research; see Harris 2007:143–67.) However, they suffered steady losses and Che grew increasingly ill since he had no medicine to treat his frequent severe asthma attacks. At the end of August, the guerrilla column under Joaquín (Che's Cuban comrade Comandante Juan Vitalio Acuña Nuñez) was ambushed and all but one member of the column were killed by the army. Among the losses was the guerrilla force's only female member, Tania (Tamara Bunke). By the middle of September, the remaining column under Che's command was being encircled by an increasing number of troops, and the news of the army's successful encounters in late September with his column near La Higuera, a small hamlet of about 100 inhabitants 90 miles Southwest of the city of Santa Cruz, was received by the military high command and the government of President Barrientos as a clear sign victory was almost within their grasp. In Vallegrande, the main town in this area, the new Second Manchego Ranger Regiment had just arrived after fi nishing 19 weeks of special counterinsurgency training from U.S. Army Special Forces personnel. By dawn on September 27, the fi rst units of this new regiment had moved into the region around La Higuera. A unit of these U.S.-trained Rangers captured one of the Bolivian members of Che's guerrillas force who was code-named Camba (his real name was Orlando Jiménez Bazán) and was able to interrogate another Bolivian member of Che's column named León (Antonio Rodríguez Flores), who had deserted the guerrilla force and turned himself over to the army following a particularly bloody engagement in which several members of Che's force were killed.

In his diary, Che acknowledged his losses were very great in the La Higuera area, particularly the death of three of his best comrades. He considered the loss of his Bolivian lieutenant Coco (Roberto Peredo Leigue, who had been trained in Cuba and Vietnam) the most grievous loss. In addition, he noted in his diary that his Cuban comrade Miguel (Manuel Hernández, who had been with him since 1958) and the Bolivian doctor with the code name Julio (Mario Gutierrez Ardaya) had been magnifi cent fi ghters and the human value of all three was inexpressible. His diary also reveals that the last days of September were extremely tense ones for him and his men. They were forced to move by night and hide during the day, and on more than one occasion they were nearly discovered by the soldiers who were searching for them.

By the end of the month, it was clear to everyone in Che's small force they were in a desperate position. A circle of troops was closing in around them, and their every move was being reported to the army by the local population. Their tragic plight was summed up cryptically by Che in his diary: "Our conditions are the same as last month, except now the army is demonstrating increasing effectiveness in its actions and the campesinos are giving us no support and have turned into informers."

Nevertheless, Che still believed they could continue their mission. Thus, he noted in his diary: "The most important task is to escape and look for more propitious zones; and then afterwards our contacts, in spite of the fact that the whole apparatus is disrupted in La Paz where they have given us severe blows." In view of the circumstances, however, Che and his comrades had little chance "to escape and look for more propitious zones." They were completely surrounded by thousands of troops and unable to move rapidly across the diffi cult terrain owing to their wounds and fatigue.

T hroughout the fi rst few days of October, Che and his group, now reduced to 16, spent most of the daylight hours on the crests of the ridges north of La Higuera and the nights in the hollows at the bases of these ridges. On the evening of October 3, Che heard a news broadcast concerning Camba and León, and he made the following entry in his diary: "Both gave abundant information about Fernando [Che's own code name], his illness and everything else." Che added sarcastically: "Thus ends the story of two heroic guerrillas." On October 4, Che wrote that he had heard a commentary on the radio whose conclusion had been that if he was captured by troops of the Fourth Army Division, he would be tried in Camiri, but if by the Eighth Division, he would be tried in Santa Cruz.

O n Saturday, October 7, the last day Che made an entry in his diary, he and his men camped in one of the many ravines near La Higuera. There they encountered an old woman herding goats and attempted to question her about the presence of soldiers in the area, but they were unable to obtain any reliable information. Afterward, fearing that the old woman would report them, Che ordered two of his men to go to her house and pay her 50 pesos to keep quiet. He noted in his diary, however, that he had little hope that she would do as instructed. He began this last entry in his diary with a notation that it had been exactly 11 months since the inauguration of his guerrilla movement.

Apparently, the old woman or someone else who had seen Che and his group pass through the area reported their presence to the army in La Higuera. By the morning of Sunday, October 8, several companies of Rangers were deployed in the zone through which Che's small force was moving. Early that morning Captain Gary Prado and his company of Rangers, all recent graduates of the U.S. Army Special Forces training camp near Santa Cruz, took up positions on the heights of the Quebrada de Yuro, one of the most rugged ravines in the area. Che and his men, after marching the night before, had stopped to rest in this ravine until they could resume marching under cover of darkness.

A bout noon, a small probing unit from Prado's company made contact with the guerrillas. In this initial encounter, two soldiers were killed and several others wounded. The lieutenant in charge of the unit radioed Captain Prado for assistance. The subsequent series of events reads like a scenario out of a U.S. Army counterinsurgency manual. Captain Prado immediately deployed the rest of his troops in a circle around the guerrillas. Meanwhile, Che divided his small force into two groups in an effort to confuse the Rangers and escape. The group led by Che moved toward the closest exit from the ravine. However, the hill commanding this exit was occupied by a sizable number of troops and had been chosen by Captain Prado as the site of his command post. As Che and his group came within shooting range of Prado's men, they found themselves caught in a rain of automatic weapons fi re.

Captain Prado watched the guerrillas disperse and run for cover through his fi eld glasses and ordered Sergeant Bernardino Huanca and his men to descend in pursuit. A few minutes later, Sergeant Huanca fi red a burst from his submachine gun at a guerrilla moving through a thicket of thorn bushes. One bullet sent the guerrilla's black beret fl ying off his head, while two others tore into his leg and forced him to the ground. The fallen guerrilla was Che. As he lay helpless the Rangers began to concentrate their fi re on the area where he had fallen. But Willy (Simón Cuba, one of Moisés Guevara's recruits whom Che had begun to regard as a potential deserter) rushed to his side and helped him out of the line of fi re and up one side of the ravine. As the two scrambled upward, they ran into four Rangers who were positioning a mortar. The Rangers ordered them to surrender, but Che, supporting himself against a tree, fi red his carbine in answer. The soldiers returned the fi re. A few seconds later, a bullet hit the barrel of Che's carbine, rendering it useless and wounding him in the right forearm. At this point, Che reportedly raised his hands and shouted: "Don't shoot! I'm Che Guevara, and I'm worth more to you alive than dead." A few yards away, Willy threw down his rifl e and also surrendered.

I t was approximately 4:00 in the afternoon when Che and Willy were brought before Captain Prado. The latter immediately ordered his radio operator to signal the divisional headquarters in Vallegrande and tell them that they had captured Che Guevara. When the radio operator established contact with Vallegrande he shouted: "Hello, Saturno, we have Papa!" ("Saturno" was the code name for Colonel Joaquín Zenteno, commandant of the Eighth Bolivian Army Division, and "Papa" was the code name they used for Che). In disbelief, Colonel Zenteno asked Captain Prado to confi rm the message. Following the confi rmation, there was general euphoria among Colonel Zenteno's divisional headquarters staff. When the back patting subsided, Colonel Zenteno radioed Prado to immediately bring Che and any other prisoners to La Higuera.

Since the Rangers had come into the Quebrada de Yuro on foot, Che had to be transported the seven kilometers to La Higuera stretched out in a blanket carried by four soldiers. Willy was forced to walk behind with his hands tied against his back. They arrived in La Higuera shortly after dark. The prisoners were placed in the little town's two-room schoolhouse, Che in one room and Willy in the other. Later the Rangers brought in a third guerrilla, a Bolivian named Aniceto (Aniceto Reinaga), who had been taken prisoner near where Che and Willy were captured. He was placed in the classroom with Willy. The bodies of four other guerrillas were also brought to La Higuera that night.

The remaining group of guerrillas, led by Inti Peredo, had gone to the opposite end of the Quebrada when Che ordered the column to separate. They were able to hide until nightfall and then slip out of the ravine. In subsequent weeks, half the members of this second group were killed by the army. Of those who survived, the three remaining Cubans fl ed the country via Chile, and the three surviving Bolivians who included Inti went into hiding.

A. uring the night of October 8, and the next morning, Che was in-terrogated by various army offi cers, including Major Miguel Ayoroa, Colonel Andrés Selich, Captain Prado, and Colonel Zenteno. He was also questioned by the CIA agent who called himself Félix Ramos (Félix Rodríguez), one of the Cuban exiles sent by the CIA to participate in the counterinsurgency campaign against the guerrillas. Che refused to answer any of their questions, but he did exchange a few words with some of the offi cers and soldiers around him. At one point, one of the younger offi cers asked Che what he was thinking about. At fi rst, Che ignored him, but when he overheard the offi cer say sarcastically to another offi cer that he (Che) was probably thinking about the immortality of the burro, Che answered: "No, I'm thinking about the immortality of the revolution." On another occasion, one of the junior offi cers, who had drunk too much in celebration of Che's capture, tried to harass him. Che responded by punching the offi cer in the face. Although Che's wounds were painful, they were not serious, and he remained conscious during this entire period.

In La Paz, President Barrientos and the high command of the Bolivian Armed Forces held an emergency meeting to decide what to do with Che. They ruled out any prospect of prosecuting him through judicial proceedings, because they reasoned a trial would focus world attention on him and present the Communists with a propaganda fi eld day. Moreover, since Bolivia did not have the death penalty, they feared that if Che remained alive as their prisoner, sympathizers from all over the world would converge on Bolivia in an effort to save him or carry on his fi ght.

They decided, therefore, that Che had to be executed immediately. Moreover, they decided that they would announce he had died from wounds received in battle.

Early on the morning of Monday, October 9, the top-ranking offi cers in La Higuera received the order from La Paz to execute Che. They in turn instructed the noncommissioned offi cers present to carry out the order. Since none of the latter were anxious to do so, they chose lots to determine who would execute Che. Several hours before, these noncommissioned offi cers, as well as the offi cers and the soldiers on guard around the schoolhouse where Che was being held prisoner, had divided among themselves the money and personal effects taken from Che after his capture. His watches, carbine, compass, Parker fountain pen, two berets (including the one with a bullet hole through it), belt, stainless steel dagger, two pipes, and cigarette holder were the most important pieces of booty distributed among those who had had the honor of participating in the capture of the famous guerrilla leader.

S hortly before noon on Monday, October 9, 1967, some 24 hours after Che and his men had been discovered in the Quebrada de Yuro, Sergeant Mario Terán walked to the little schoolhouse in La Higuera to carry out the order sent down from the Bolivian government's top leaders in La Paz. He had drawn the shortest straw. When he entered the classroom where his victim was waiting, he found him propped up against one of the walls. Che guessed the nature of Sergeant Terán's mission and calmly asked him to wait a moment until he stood up. Terán was so frightened by the prospect of what he had to do that he began to tremble. He turned and ran from the schoolhouse. But both Colonel Selich and Colonel Zenteno ordered him to go back and shoot Che without further delay. Still trembling, Terán returned to the classroom, and without looking at his victim's face, he fi red a burst from his carbine. The bullets slammed into Che's chest and side, passed through his body, and made large holes in the soft adobe wall of the classroom. The sergeant had been told not to infl ict any wounds in Che's head or heart so that the army could later claim that he had died from wounds received in combat. However, while Terán's carbine was still smoking, several soldiers pushed past him into the classroom. They said that they too wanted to shoot Che so that they could boast that they had shot the famous Che Guevara. Sergeant Terán weakly nodded his approval and they began fi ring.

When the shooting was over, there were nine bullet wounds in Che's body, two of which were obviously instantaneously fatal. Moments later, Willy and Aniceto were executed by another sergeant in Captain Prado's company. The shooting resounded through the streets of the village, startling the townspeople and causing them to crowd around the little schoolhouse. In a short time, the entire town knew what had taken place there.

S oon after Che and his comrades were shot, the senior army offi cers and the CIA agent, Félix Rodríguez, left La Higuera by helicopter for the army headquarters in Vallegrande. Che's body was wrapped in canvas and strapped to the runner of a helicopter bound for Vallegrande. At the Vallegrande airstrip, nearly half the population of the town awaited the arrival of Che's body. Colonel Zenteno had announced several hours earlier that Che was dead and would soon be brought to Vallegrande.

W hen the helicopter arrived in Vallegrande, it landed on the side of the airstrip away from the waiting crowd of townspeople, reporters, and soldiers. Before the rotor of the helicopter had stopped, Che's body was loaded into the back of a white Chevrolet panel truck (the type used at the time as ambulances throughout most of Latin America) and transported at high speed through Vallegrande's narrow streets to the Señor de Malta Hospital.

The body was placed in an adobe laundry shack apart from the main hospital building. In this shack several offi cials washed the blood from

Che's body, made an incision in his neck for embalming fl uid, and took his fi ngerprints. According to two British journalists who arrived on the scene early, the entire process appeared to be under the supervision of a CIA agent who called himself Dr. Eduardo González (Gustavo Villoldo). He refused to let the two journalists photograph Che, and when they asked him in English where he was from, he answered sarcastically: "From nowhere!"

S oon General Alfredo Ovando, head of the Bolivian Armed Forces, and a number of other top military fi gures came to see the body of the famous guerrilla. By this time, a large crowd had excitedly collected around the shack. They probably would have broken through the cordon of soldiers trying to hold them back had it not been for the quick intervention of General Ovando. The general explained that they all had a right to see Che but that they would have to wait until the doctors and other offi cials had fi nished preparing and identifying the body.

O nce the doctors and the offi cials had fi nished their work, the soldiers allowed the waiting newsmen to enter the shack and take pictures. Afterward, they let townspeople fi le past to view the corpse. Throughout the night a silent fi le of staring townspeople, peasants from the surrounding area, and soldiers passed by the body. Che's body was on a stretcher that had been placed across the length of a concrete laundry sink. He was nude from the waist up—the offi cials had removed his jacket during the preceding investigation and preparation. The bullet wounds in his chest and sides were almost inconspicuous. He looked amazingly alive. Not only were his eyes open and brilliant but there was a haunting smile on his lips. Pictures of this vibrant and serene expression were conveyed around the world by the news media.

Che's body was exhibited in the hospital at Vallegrande for approximately 24 hours. What happened to it afterward was a mystery to the world until almost 30 years later. On October 11, 1967, General Ovando fi rst stated that the body had been buried in the Vallegrande area. The next day, however, General Ovando's offi ce offi cially announced that the body had been cremated, and President Barrientos said a few days afterward that Che's ashes had been buried in a hidden place somewhere in the Vallegrande region. Almost nine months later, an article in the Peruvian paper *La Prensa* claimed that members of President Barrientos's personal guard had told a high functionary in the Peruvian police, when the Bolivian president visited Lima in July, that Che's body had been taken to the United States by the CIA in order to prevent it from falling into the hands of Marxists intent on sanctifying his remains. But a few days later, President Barrientos's personal guard publicly denied that any of its members had said anything to anyone about Che's body during the president's visit to Peru.

I n any case, the rapid disposal of the body was probably motivated by the impending arrival in La Paz of Che's brother, Roberto Guevara, who was intent on claiming the body and taking it back to Argentina. When Roberto, a lawyer, arrived in Bolivia on October 12, he was told that it was impossible for him to see his brother's body since it had been cremated the day before. Not wanting to believe that his brother had been killed, Roberto asked to see the hands that the Bolivian offi cials claimed that they had cut from the body as proof that it was really Che Guevara that they had killed. But he was denied even this request and was forced to return to Argentina without having seen any evidence that his brother died in Bolivia. However, a few days later, a team of Argentine police experts arrived in La Paz in response to an invitation by President Barrientos sent to General Onganía, the military dictator ruling Argentina at the time. The Argentine police experts were allowed to examine Che's hands and compare his fi ngerprints with those in the fi les of the Argentine Federal Police. On their departure, they issued an offi cial statement to the effect that the fi ngerprints were identical and belonged to Ernesto "Che" Guevara.

T he contradictions in the offi cial statements given by the Bolivian authorities with regard to the disposition of Che's body were minor compared to those that appeared in statements concerning how and when Che died. On October 13, Dr. José Martínez Casso, one of the two doctors at the Señor de Malta Hospital who had been asked by the military to conduct an autopsy on Che's body, reported to the press that Che had received two mortal wounds, one in the lungs and the other in the heart. He also stated that, on examining the body shortly after it had been brought to the hospital in Vallegrande, he had estimated that Che had died not more than fi ve or six hours earlier. The doctor's statements obviously indicated that Che had died from wounds he received shortly before being brought to Vallegrande, not during the battle in the Quebrada de Yuro on the previous Sunday.

Yet on the same day that Dr. Martínez Casso made his statement, Colonel Zenteno stated before a press conference that although he was not able to say precisely when Che had died, it was "almost immediately after he was wounded in combat." This was contradicted on the same day by General Ovando, who stated that Che had died early Monday morning (October 9) as a consequence of wounds received the previous afternoon in combat. Although Che could not have lived overnight with a fatal bullet wound in both his heart and lungs, General Ovando denied emphatically and indignantly the suggestion that Che had been shot to death after he was taken prisoner.

T he seemingly endless capacity of the Bolivian offi cials to contradict themselves not only made it clear that Che had been executed but also demonstrated that the government and military were incapable of discussing the matter without creating confusion and making embarrassing errors. The government's bungled efforts to sell Che's campaign diary (obtained along with other important items when he was captured in the Quebrada de Yuro), and the incredible circumstances surrounding the clandestine delivery of the diary for free to Cuba by none other than one of the top offi cials in President Barrientos's cabinet, were further evidence of the weaknesses, both moral and otherwise, in the Bolivian regime. Indeed, the entire episode involving the release of his diary had the appearance of a nightmarish comedy of errors. This tragic comedy occurred when I arrived on the scene in Bolivia some eight months after Che's death.

The success of any guerrilla movement depends on the degree of support it receives from the civilian population in its area of operations. Che knew this truth well and mentioned it frequently in his writings on guerrilla warfare.

For example, he wrote:

It is important to emphasize that the guerrilla struggle is a mass struggle, it is the struggle of a people. . . . The guerrilla fi ghter therefore relies on the complete support of the people of the area. This is absolutely indispensable. (Guevara 1960)

H owever, the complete absence of popular support for his guerrilla operation in Bolivia was one of the main reasons, if not the prime reason, that his mission there failed.

R evolutionary guerrilla warfare depends on, and is a struggle for, the loyalties of the civilian population. Close guerrilla-civilian cooperation enables guerrillas to develop a superior system of intelligence, have extreme mobility, cache an inexhaustible source of supplies, and surprise the enemy's forces when they are off guard. Without close ties to the civilian population, guerrillas cannot develop even the minimal level of capabilities necessary for successful guerrilla warfare.

REASONS FOR THE LACK OF POPULAR SUPPORT FOR CHE'S GUERRILLA MOVEMENT

One of the reasons Che's guerrilla movement failed to obtain any popular support in Bolivia is the majority of Bolivians at that time believed their country had already undergone its revolution of national liberation. Although Che visited Bolivia shortly after the revolution of 1952, he failed to perceive then or later how much importance the Bolivians attached to this event. In fact, for many Bolivians, the revolution of 1952 was regarded in much the same way as the Cubans regard their revolution. Because Che did not understand this fact, and because his Bolivian sources of information did not convey it to him, he believed his guerrilla movement would be able to capitalize on the hostility and discontent he assumed the Bolivian people felt toward their political rulers.

W hat Che failed to understand is the revolution of 1952 gave the Bolivian masses, for the fi rst time in Bolivian history, what they perceived as a real stake in the social order as well as a sense of involvement in the political system and cultural community of their country. Despite the military coup of 1964 and the consequent fall from power of the National Revolutionary Movement (the group that spearheaded the revolution of 1952 and governed the country until the military coup), the changes set in motion by the revolution had continuing relevance for most of the Bolivian population in the mid-1960s when Che and his comrades arrived on the scene. These developments had a profound impact on the character of Bolivian politics and contributed greatly to the development of a sense of national consciousness among Bolivia's rural masses.

C he failed to appreciate the importance of this national consciousness and believed the Bolivian peasantry and the workers would provide a popular base for his revolutionary guerrilla movement in Bolivia and subsequently in neighboring countries. However, conditions for creating a successful revolutionary foco were obviously not present in Bolivia in the mid-1960s. In the fi rst place, the guerrillas could not hope to win the support of the rural masses by offering to give them land. Since 1952 Bolivia's peasants had controlled the land and the entire countryside. Moreover, they had seen some improvement in their political, social, and economic status and they had hopes of greater improvement.

This is not to say that they were well off, for their situation was, and still is, one of the worst in Latin America. Nevertheless, they were much better off in the mid-1960s than they had been in the past. Furthermore, the peasants were not isolated from the centers of national political power. Through their local syndicates they had a signifi cant voice in the country's political affairs, and certain groups, such as the campesinos in the Cochabamba area, even had direct access to President Barrientos. Consequently, the leaders of the peasant syndicates and many of their members did not regard the political authorities as enemies of the people.

In view of the peasantry's increased involvement in national affairs, they perceived Che's guerrilla movement in totally different terms than he expected. Instead of supporting Che's guerrilla movement, they opposed it. For example, at the end of June 1967, the National Congress of Farm Workers issued a public declaration in which they denounced the guerrillas as an "anti-national force, fi nanced from abroad and destined to create nothing but confusion and disruption." This group further stated that they were ready to cooperate with the armed forces "in totally liquidating this foreign aggression that is attempting to undermine in a systematic manner the economic and social development of our people."

T hat the Bolivian public perceived the guerrillas as foreigners seriously handicapped the guerrilla movement. Saddled with this stigma, it was impossible for them to win widespread popular support among the general population. In fact, certain Bolivian observers referred to the foreign character of Che's guerrilla movement as its "original sin." Since the guerrilla operation was neither organized nor led by Bolivians, it aroused a nationalistic reaction among nearly every segment of Bolivian society. The foreign character of the guerrilla operation also made it possible for President Barrientos and the Bolivian military to wrap themselves in the Bolivian fl ag and play the role of defenders of the Bolivian nation.

Even if Che's group had not been marked with the stigma of "foreign intruders," it seems highly unlikely they would have been able to establish a base of popular support among the peasantry in the southeast of Bolivia. The peasantry would not have been receptive to any type of armed uprising. The fact that Che and his group were considered foreigners, of course, made it impossible for them to develop an armed uprising among the rural population, and so they found themselves isolated and surrounded on all sides by informers and government sympathizers.

U.S. INVOLVEMENT IN THE DEFEAT OF CHE'S GUERRILLA FORCE

S ensationalist claims that the U.S. Central Intelligence Agency (CIA) brought down Che have no factual foundation at all. To be sure, the CIA was ever present during the entire episode; they certainly were determined to see that Che was defeated and, if possible, captured. However, they were not responsible for the failure of Che's guerrilla operation or his execution. In fact, the U.S. government and the CIA appear to have opposed the idea of executing Che. Purely for professional reasons, the CIA wanted to keep him alive. This appears to have been the position of the U.S. government from the highest levels down to the two CIA agents on the scene. Thus, in his (now declassifi ed) memorandum to President Lyndon Johnson confi rming the death of Che Guevara, Walt Rostow (who was the president's special assistant for National Security Affairs) told the president the following:

C IA tells us that the latest information is Guevara was taken alive. After a short interrogation to establish his identity, General Ovando—Chief of the Bolivian Armed Forces—ordered him shot. I regard this as stupid, but it is understandable from a Bolivian standpoint given the problems which the sparing of French Communist and Castro courier Regis Debray has caused them.

R ostow also provides in this memorandum his analysis of the "signifi cant implications" of Che's death. He wrote:

- I t marks the passing of another of the aggressive, romantic rev-olutionaries like Sukarno, Nkrumah, Ben Bella . . . and reinforces this trend.
- In the Latin American context, it will have a strong impact in discouraging would-be guerrillas.
- I t shows the soundness of our "preventive medicine" assistance to countries facing incipient insurgency—it was the Bolivian 2nd Ranger Battalion, trained by our Green Berets from June– September of this year that cornered and got him.

R ostow closed the memorandum with the comment that he had "put these points across to several newsmen" (Rostow 1967).

G ustavo Villoldo, one of the two CIA agents on the scene at Che's capture, claims: "At no time did I or the CIA have a say in executing Che . . . that was a Bolivian decision" (Tamayo 1997). The other CIA agent present was Félix Rodríguez, who later became the president of the militant Cuban-exile organization Brigade 2506. He has claimed repeatedly he was under CIA instructions to "do everything possible to keep him alive," but Rodríguez has also admitted he transmitted the order to execute Guevara that came by radio from the Bolivian high command to the soldiers at La Higuera. And he also claims he directed them not to shoot Guevara in the face so that his wounds would appear to be combat related (*Miami's Cuban Connection* 2006).

Rodríguez contends he personally informed Che that he would be killed. He told *Miami's Cuban Connection* in a 2006 interview: "I walked in and gave the order to untie him. Che had asked if we could untie him and let him sit down. Later, the order came from the Bolivian government to shoot him. I tried in all my power to stop them because of my instructions to take him to Panama for the CIA. . . . At the end, I asked him if he wanted me to do something for his family. He said 'Tell my wife to marry again and try to be happy.' We shook hands, hugged. I left the room and someone came in and shot him." Later in this interview he said it was Sergeant Mario Terán who shot Che. After Che was executed, Rodríguez claims he took Che's Rolex watch, which he has proudly shown reporters over the years.

I f the CIA agents advised the Bolivians to keep Che alive, this advice was clearly rejected by the Bolivian government's top leaders, who felt they could not afford to allow the famous revolutionary to live. Bolivia had no death penalty, so they were afraid an imprisoned Che would become a cause célèbre that would attract leftists to the country from around the world. Moreover, if they turned him over to the CIA, they would give the world and the Bolivian people the impression the U.S. government was running things in Bolivia. They felt they had no other choice politically but to execute Che. They also decided to cover this up by claiming he died after capture from wounds received in battle.

Exaggerated claims about U.S. involvement in the defeat of Che's guerrilla force have also been made with regard to the use of infrared aerial cameras by U.S. planes to detect and locate the guerrillas. One journalist in particular asserted the mud ovens used by the guerrillas made it possible for the U.S. Air Force to pinpoint their location at all times by using new, highly sensitive heat-detecting cameras in an around-

the-clock aerial surveillance of the combat zone. However, after leaving their main camp in the Ñancahuazú area, where they did have a mud oven, the guerrillas never stayed anywhere long enough to build another one. In fact, they rarely even built fi res.

Furthermore, the Bolivian authorities knew at least the general location of the guerrillas throughout the entire period from their initial discovery to their elimination in October. They did not have to rely on such sophisticated American gimmickry as heat-sensing infrared cameras. For one thing, during the fi rst four months of operations, Che's column clashed with the army fairly frequently, and it was possible to ascertain simply from these encounters their general location. Moreover, the army constantly received information about them from the local peasantry. In fact, the irony of the situation is that the Bolivian military knew far more about the guerrillas than the latter knew about the army—the exact reversal of the usual situation in guerrilla warfare.

In sum, the U.S. involvement in Bolivian affairs was extensive, but the U.S. contribution to the military defeat of Che's guerrilla operation was minimal and then only at the end. To be sure, the U.S. trained the Rangers of the Second Manchego Rangers Regiment who were responsible for capturing Che and almost completely eliminating his small force in October 1967. However, Che's guerrilla operation was already defeated prior to the arrival on the scene of the U.S.-trained Rangers. His force had lost over half of its original members and had failed to win any popular support. Moreover, the hostility of the pro-Soviet Communist Party leaders and the indifference of the other leftist groups in Bolivia, together with the capture of the guerrillas' urban contacts in La Paz, had left Che and the tattered remnants of his original force completely and hopelessly isolated by the time the Rangers entered into combat against them.

Che's Diary and Hidden Remains

Following Che's capture and execution, the Barrientos government decided to sell Che's diary to the publisher willing to pay the highest price (the information in this chapter is based on the author's original research; see Harris 2007:227–56). However, while the Bolivians were negotiating the sale of the diary, the Cuban government mysteriously obtained a copy and released it through publishing houses in Latin America, Europe, and the United States. By publishing the diary before the Bolivians could sell it, the Cuban government was able to score a signifi cant propaganda victory and greatly embarrass the Barrientos regime. Moreover, the questions about how the Cubans got a copy of the diary gave rise to serious doubts in Bolivia about the integrity of the government and the armed forces. Clearly, someone in the civilian side of the government or the military had placed a copy of this top-secret document in the hands of the Cuban government.

C he's diary was made public in Havana on July 1, 1968, shortly after I had arrived in La Paz, and within a few days it was distributed by leftist publishers in Chile, Mexico, France, Italy, West Germany, and the United States. A few weeks later, on July 17, Antonio Arguedas, Minister of the Interior and a close friend of President Barrientos, fl ed to Chile and was denounced by General Ovando as the traitor who had provided the Cuban government with photographic copies of Che's diary. The Bolivian public was stunned by the news, and most of the population regarded Arguedas's actions as a national disgrace.

S ince Arguedas had been President Barrientos's right-hand man, the whole affair seriously undermined the public's confi dence in the Barrientos regime and within 24 hours plunged the country into a grave political crisis that broke apart the coalition of political parties that had previously supported Barrientos. At the same time, the three main opposition parties (the rightwing Socialist Falange, the centrist National Revolutionary Movement, and the Trotskyist Revolutionary Party of the Nationalist Left) issued a manifesto calling on the Barrientos government to resign. They also called a mass demonstration in the capital on July 20, which resulted in a violent clash with the police and the death of a captain of the Civil Guard.

The leaders of the demonstration were arrested, and Barrientos declared a nationwide state of emergency. He also called on the peasant syndicates in the Cochabamba area to come to his assistance, and 5,000 armed campesinos from the Cochabamba Valley were mobilized and moved to the outskirts of La Paz. This appears to have been the turning point in the crisis. Soon thereafter Barrientos received expressions of public support from the various military garrisons throughout the country, as well as several important political groups. Ironically, the crisis arising from the publication of Che's diary, and particularly Arguedas's part in the whole affair, almost toppled the

Barrientos regime—something Che's guerrilla operation never came close to achieving while he was alive.

But the Arguedas affair did not end there. Much to everyone's surprise, approximately a month after his fl ight from the country, Antonio Arguedas voluntarily returned to Bolivia to stand trial for his actions. In Chile Arguedas had publicly declared that he wanted to return to Bolivia to clear his name. However, most Bolivians assumed he had received a large sum of money from the Cubans in return for Che's diary, so no one took seriously his announced intention to return home. This made it all the more surprising when he did return to Bolivia, following a monthlong odyssey that took him to Buenos Aires, Madrid, London, New York, and Lima, before arriving back in La Paz.

When he arrived in Bolivia, Arguedas told the press that he had returned in order to clear his conscience and face the consequences of his past actions. His exact words to the Bolivian press were the following:

I am not looking for publicity. I only want to tell the truth about everything that occurred in my career as a subsecretary and minister of government, and alert not only the present government of Bolivia, but all the governments of Latin America, as to how North American imperialism undermines their intelligence services in order to introduce errors, to distort, to present a completely different picture of reality, to obstruct their economic relations with other states, and fi nally to keep them under its control.

H e said he had returned in order to regain his personal dignity by telling the truth at the moment when it was most appropriate to do so. In this regard, he reminded the reporters he had been the favorite of both the Americans and the most reactionary political elements in Bolivia prior to his sending Che's diary to Fidel Castro, and that he had given up a promising political career because of his disgust over the undermining of Bolivia's national sovereignty by U.S. political and economic interests.

A t the press conference following his return to Bolivia, Arguedas refuted the suggestion that he had given a copy of Che's diary to Fidel Castro because he was a Castroite or because he was a Communist. He denied being either a Castroite or a Communist and stated that he was a nationalist fi rst and a Marxist second. With regard to the accusation that he had received a large sum of money for the diary, Arguedas angrily retorted that this was another of the CIA's insidious attempts to discredit him by slander. He argued that if it had been money he was after, it would have been unnecessary for him to sell Che's diary to the Cubans. Arguedas pointed out that as minister of internal affairs he could have made a fortune in bribes from the Americans if he had wanted to do so. He said he had documents hidden outside the country that, among other things, proved that a U.S. engineering fi rm (which he named) had offered him a bribe of $1.5 million to see that they were awarded a government contract for the construction of two new highways. In other words, he argued that he had rejected bribes of much greater amounts than the $500,000 it was rumored he had received from the Cubans for the diary.

T he Arguedas affair is one consequence of Che's guerrilla operation that Che himself could never have foreseen. Arguedas's actions shook the Barrientos regime to the core, whereas Che's guerrilla activities, at least before the Arguedas affair, had the effect of strengthening the Barrientos regime and the Bolivian military. By calling into question the integrity of the government and the armed forces, Arguedas's actions weakened the Barrientos regime and the public's confi dence in the existing political system. Moreover, Arguedas's return to Bolivia and his revelations about the nature of the CIA's interference in Bolivian affairs called into question the role of the United States government and companies in that country. In fact, the Arguedas affair provides shocking evidence about the nature of the U.S. government's involvement in the domestic affairs of Latin American countries.

F ollowing his press conference in the Ministry of the Interior the day of his return to Bolivia, Arguedas was placed in strict confi nement and not allowed to make any further statements to the press. However, within a few months he was released from prison as a result of the Bolivian high court's decision that it did not have the authority to try him. According to the high court, the Bolivian legislature was the only body competent to try a former minister of state for acts of treason committed while in offi ce. Because of the court's decision, Arguedas was released from prison pending action by the legislature.

H e kept a low profi le after his release, but within a short time several attempts were made on his life. Twice bombs were thrown at him, and on June 6, 1969, he and a Spanish journalist accompanying him were machine-gunned while walking on the street in La Paz. Both Arguedas and the journalist escaped with minor wounds. However, Arguedas was hospitalized for almost a month, and immediately following his release from the hospital, he sought asylum in the Mexican embassy.

In a statement he gave to the press at the time, he explained that his intentions were to leave Bolivia and go to Mexico. He said that he had decided to leave Bolivia because of the increasing political instability in the country following the death of President Barrientos (who was killed when his personal helicopter crashed in mysterious circumstances) and because of the recent attempts on his life. He gave as an additional reason the failure of the government to take any action whatsoever against the agents of U.S. imperialism who were at work undermining Bolivia's national sovereignty.

D uring this time, Arguedas was the author of yet another incredible episode. He secretly arranged for Che's hands, in a glass container of formaldehyde, and a plaster mask of his face (made in Vallegrande) to be sent to Cuba in much the same manner as he had arranged for the copies of Che's diary to be sent there. However, in this case, the existence and transfer of these items to Cuba were not discovered until many years later. In fact, to this day, the story of Che's hands and his death mask is not widely known.

CHE'S HANDS AND DEATH MASK

T he odyssey of these two items is more complex and more diffi cult to follow than the story of Che's diary. The man who cut off Che's hands and made his death mask out of plaster was Roberto "Toto" Quintanilla, an offi cial in Arguedas's ministry. Like many of the other fi gures associated with Che's death, he was killed under unusual circumstances in November 1970. An unknown woman gunned him down with an automatic weapon in his offi ce in Hamburg, Germany, where he was serving as the Bolivian consul. Nothing more is known about him than this. According to Arguedas, Che's hands and his death mask were given to him by General Ovando after they had been inspected by the team of Argentine criminal investigators sent to Bolivia to verify Che's fi ngerprints.

G eneral Ovando instructed Arguedas to dispose of both items immediately and to leave no traces of them. However, Arguedas chose to ignore Ovando's orders and gave them for safekeeping to a close friend named Jorge Suarez, a Bolivian writer and the editor of the daily newspaper *Jornada.* In a little known interview that Suarez gave Argentine journalist Uki Goñi in 1995, Suarez claimed Arguedas asked him to come to his offi ce seven or eight days after Che's death. Arguedas told him he wanted to discuss something very personal and urgent. When Suarez went to his offi ce, Arguedas produced a glass container and a translucent bag, the contents of both Suarez could not at fi rst see clearly. After Arguedas motioned for him to come closer and examine the two objects, Suarez saw two hands fl oating in the glass container and he saw a white plaster mask in the bag. As he studied the mask closely he saw that it was an extraordinarily good replica of Che's face with his eyes open. He could even see the details of his beard. It did not appear to be the face of someone dead, rather of someone very much alive. Suarez told Goñi he would never forget that face (Goñi 1995).

Arguedas explained to Suarez that General Ovando had given him strict instructions to incinerate the hands and the mask and then scatter the ashes in a river, but that he had decided not to follow these orders. He asked Suarez to take the items with him and hide them in his home. Although he was shocked and frightened, Suarez agreed to do what his friend asked him. According to Suarez, Arguedas said he was an admirer of Che and that the top levels of the Bolivian military and the U.S. embassy as well as certain other infl uential people did not trust him. In fact, he said the U.S. embassy suspected him of being a revolutionary and a possible contact for the guerrillas. By not destroying the death mask and Che's hands Arguedas said that he was risking his life.

Suarez made a sort of sarcophagus, or stone coffi n, for the items under the fl oor of his bedroom and hid them there. Although his house was searched several times by the Bolivian secret police while Arguedas was in prison, Che's hands and death mask were not discovered. They stayed under the fl oor in his bedroom until Suarez left Bolivia in 1969 as the new ambassador to Mexico, appointed by the military government of none other than General Ovando. Suarez told Goñi (1995) that the Bolivian intelligence services and the CIA concluded afterward that he had probably carried Che's hands and death mask out of the country in his diplomatic pouch, so they discontinued looking for them. However, he had left them hidden under the fl oor of his bedroom.

M eanwhile, following his release from prison, Arguedas sought refuge in the Mexican embassy while his request for political exile to Mexico was under consideration. When he learned that Suarez was leaving the country for Mexico, he made arrangements to have Che's hands and death mask taken to Cuba in much the same way he had arranged for Che's diary to be taken. In July 1969, he asked his journalist friend Víctor Zannier to arrange for the two items to be sent to Cuba. Zannier in turn delegated the mission to Jorge Sattori and Juan Coronel. Although they were members of the pro-Soviet Bolivian Communist Party, Zannier felt they could be trusted, and he fi gured they could use the party's international connections to get out of the country and travel to Cuba. Juan Coronel kept the glass container with Che's hands and the bag with his death mask wrapped up in old newspapers under his bed for fi ve months while he and Sattori made their arrangements to go to Cuba by way of Europe and the Soviet Union.

Coronel was struck by how much the death mask revealed Che's features, and he described the glass container as cylindrical, about 10 inches high and 7 inches wide, and sealed with red wax. Inside were two hands fl oating in a brownish liquid. They appeared to have belonged to someone who had been quite strong. He said they were covered in a beautiful fi lm (most likely the ink used to record Che's fi ngerprints), and they appeared to have been amputated with an inadequate instrument that left an irregular cut just before the wrists. Coronel's description of the way the hands were amputated matches the image in the shocking photographs of Che's hands that were taken by the Argentine criminal investigators who were sent to Bolivia to prove that the Bolivian military had indeed captured and killed the famous Che Guevara. Their story and the photos they took were not released until many years later (De Carlos 2006). In their photographs, Che's hands are seen palm up on a newspaper page with the curled fi ngers covered in ink and the ink bottle and pad next to them.

ARGUEDAS'S ODYSSEY

The Mexican embassy arranged for Arguedas to leave Bolivia and go to Mexico in 1969, where I met him briefl y at a conference in Cuernavaca. He appeared to be quite happy in Mexico. However, he subsequently left Mexico for Cuba, where he was celebrated for his actions (Anderson 1997:745) and lived for nine years. While he was living in Havana, he was visited several times by Antonio Peredo

(Estellano 2000), the oldest brother of Coco and Inti. Peredo is a well-known Bolivian journalist, political activist, and university professor. According to Peredo, Arguedas lived a very disciplined and studious existence while he was in Cuba, and he regularly spent his days doing research in the libraries.

I n 1979 Arguedas returned to Bolivia and disappeared from public view. In the mid-1980s, his name appeared again in the press because he was accused of being involved in an armed group that kidnapped a wealthy businessman. Although his involvement in this affair was never proved conclusively, he was arrested and remained in prison from 1986 to 1989. After his release, he dropped out of sight again and did not surface until 1997, the year the search for Che's remains in Bolivia reached a crescendo and became a highly publicized international effort. During this period, the media and some of the people involved in the search for Che's remains tried to locate Arguedas to see if he could tell them where Che's body had been buried. However, the police found Arguedas fi rst and arrested him for supposedly leading a gang that was planning to kidnap businessmen in order to extract ransom money from their families and business associates. He was released by the police while awaiting trial, and he immediately went into hiding. Subsequently, he was declared a fugitive from justice when he failed to appear in court on the date of his trial.

D uring this time, he told Antonio Peredo that he had in his possession the names of everyone involved in the drug trade in Bolivia, and that many people knew this. For this reason, he told Peredo: "I'm a dangerous man" (Estellano 2000). By this time, the Bolivian police were trying to link him to a series of bombings in La Paz. They arrested three men who they said belonged to a terrorist group that was led by Arguedas, but they were unable to present any serious proof that he was involved in this group.

B etween November 20 and December 16, 1999, there were six bombings in random locations around La Paz that made no sense and that were never explained by the police. The police accused Antonio Arguedas of being responsible for the bombings and for the deaths of several people who were killed by the bombings. He did not turn himself into the authorities and remained in hiding.

In February 2000, the police reported that he was killed in La Paz when a bomb he was carrying exploded. The police said he belonged to a right-wing group called C-4, which had declared war against Castroism, drugs, and corruption in Bolivia. But Arguedas's family members and local political observers expressed serious doubts about the police account of his death (Estellano 2000). It remains unclear whether his death was accidental or intentional. One newspaper account suggested that the police explanation of Arguedas's death provided an ironic metaphor for his zigzagging political life. According to this account, instead of moving the timer on the bomb to the right to start its timing sequence, he moved it to the contact point on the left, and it instantly blew up in his hands (*Clarín.com* 2000). Of course, it is more likely he was killed by the police. The true story of his death may never be known.

CHE'S BODY

As for Che's body, after it was displayed in Vallegrande it disappeared from public view and became a state secret.

Since the Bolivian military refused to give any information to the public about this subject, there was considerable speculation about what happened to it. Some people believed the CIA had taken Che's body back to the United States, others that his body had been cremated and his ashes spread over the jungle by air, and some thought he was buried in a secret location. It now appears that the CIA agent Gustavo Villoldo was responsible for burying Che's body in an unmarked grave near the Vallegrande airport along with six of Che's former companions in arms. At least this is where his bones were ultimately uncovered.

Thirty years after his death and following an almost 2-year search, in July 1997 a team of Cuban and Argentine experts found his remains with those of six of his comrades in an unmarked grave at the edge of the Vallegrande airport. The Cuban-Argentine team conclusively identifi ed one of the skeletons as being Che's remains on the basis of its facial bone structure, teeth, and absence of hands (Rother 1997). It also was found with a jacket and was not wearing socks, consistent with the last photographs taken of Che after he was killed, which show him lying on a jacket and without socks.

The search for and discovery of Che's remains in Bolivia adds yet another page to the remarkable story of his life and death and reveals that his legacy continues to take on new dimensions as time passes. On November 26, 1995, the *New York Times* published an article containing statements of retired Bolivian army general Mario Vargas Salinas to the effect that Che's body had been buried under the landing strip at the Vallegrande airport (Castañeda 1997:404–5). In fact, the widow of Colonel Andrés Selich told the journalist Jon Lee Anderson, who was collecting information for his biographical book on Che Guevara, that her husband and a couple of other Bolivian army offi cers (including Vargas) had buried Che's body and the bodies of six of his comrades in two unmarked graves dug by a bulldozer near the Vallegrande airport (Anderson 1997:742). When Anderson questioned Vargas (who wrote a book in 1988 about Che's Bolivian operation), he told Anderson that all the bodies had been buried in one unmarked grave near the edge of the airport. The reporting of these details of Che's death, especially in the *New York Times* by Thomas Lipscomb (November 26, 1995:3), caused a political uproar in Bolivia. It also stirred a great deal of interest in the international media and gave rise to a fl ood of new information about Che's death and his fatal Bolivian mission.

U nder pressure from the national and the international press, the president of Bolivia ordered the army to recover the bodies of Che and his comrades. What followed was a rather bizarre and highly publicized search for their bodies by an odd assortment of Bolivians, Cubans, and Argentines, which attracted many onlookers and reporters (Anderson 1997:xv). The whole affair turned out to be a source of considerable embarrassment for the Bolivian government and military since it resurrected a controversial chapter in Bolivia's political history. For his part in the whole affair, Vargas was placed under house arrest for revealing state secrets.

T he little town of Vallegrande, with a population of approximately 8,000 people, was in the news again, but this time because of the presence of Cuban forensic anthropologists and geologists. At fi rst, they located the remains of only 5 of the guerrillas, a fraction of the 32 guerrillas who were killed in the area and buried in unmarked graves. But for 16 months there was no sign of

Che's body.

Meanwhile, Vallegrande's municipal government leaders declared Che's remains were a "national patrimony" and imposed a moratorium on the search until mid-June 1997. Someone in the town also started promoting a $70 per day walking tour of the route taken by Che and his comrades before they were caught and killed, and there was talk of creating a museum. Loyola Guzman, who had been the treasurer of the clandestine urban network that supported Che's guerrilla force before she and the others were arrested and imprisoned by the Bolivian authorities, stated publicly that Che's remains should rightfully remain in Bolivian soil. She argued that "his life was an example of heroic internationalism that no single country should monopolize." Following her release from prison, Guzman returned to leftist activism and was very much involved in the campaign for the defense of human rights in Bolivia. In 2006 she was elected to the Constituent Assembly in Bolivia as one of the representatives of the Movimiento al Socialismo (MAS, or Movement toward Socialism). In Che's diary, he noted that "Loyola made a very good impression on me. She is very young and sweet, but one notes a strong determination."

THE DISCOVERY OF CHE'S BODY

T he Cuban team met until 4 a.m. on June 28, 1997, before they decided where to focus their day of digging, according to Alejandro Inchaurregui, one of a team of Argentine forensic anthropologists who were called in to help the Cubans (Tamayo 1997). Ground radar surveys made by the Cuban-Argentine search team earlier in 1997 had discovered a dozen spots of disturbed earth that they thought could be grave sites. Three of these sites appeared to be human made, and they decided to concentrate on these sites using a bulldozer—not the preferred tool of forensic specialists. However, time was running out for the CubanArgentine team of experts because of changing political circumstances in Bolivia.

T hey set the blade of the bulldozer to remove four inches of dirt with each pass of the blade. They found nothing at the fi rst site, but at the second site after 18 passes the bulldozer blade uncovered the remains of a human skeleton. As they continued to dig they found the remains of a total of seven bodies in two groups, separated by two and a half feet. The bodies were buried in a pit between the edge of Vallegrande's old dirt airstrip and a nearby cemetery. The searchers were overcome with emotion when they examined the remains of the second body that was in the middle of the fi rst group of three skeletons. The skeleton had no hands. Since they knew Che's hands had been amputated after his death, they were almost certain they had fi nally found his remains. The American author Jon Lee Anderson was present during the digging on this day, and according to Anderson: "Just seeing the genuine excitement, the genuine euphoria on the face of the Cubans there [made] me certain this was Che's remains . . . they were simply overcome, crying and hugging each other" (Tamayo 1997).

However, they still had to prove to the Bolivian government that the remains were those of Che and obtain permission to send them to Cuba. According to the Argentine forensic anthropologist Inchaurregui, the Bolivian Ministry of Interior offi cials had warned them they needed to move fast, since the inauguration of Bolivia's newly elected right-wing president and former military dictator, Hugo Banzer, was rapidly approaching and they assumed he would likely block the removal of Che's remains. Thus, on the night of July 5, 1997, a convoy of vehicles with the remains of the guerrillas made the 150-mile trip at full speed along the dangerous mountain roads between Vallegrande and the provincial capital of Santa Cruz.

In Santa Cruz, Che's remains were quickly identifi ed. The team of examiners was composed of experts from the Institute of Forensic Medicine in Havana, the director of Che's personal archive María del Carmen Ariet and the Argentine forensic anthropologists. They matched the evidence of bullet wounds in the bones of Skeleton 2 with the historical facts of Che's death. The excavated teeth of Skeleton 2 matched a plaster mold of Che's teeth made in Cuba before he left for the Congo. The mold had been made in the event he died in combat and his body had to be identifi ed. Moreover, there was other evidence to support the conclusion that the remains were indeed those of Che Guevara.

For example, retired Bolivian Air Force General Jaime Nino de Guzman, the helicopter pilot who fl ew Che's body and the bodies of the other guerrillas killed in or near La Higuera to Vallegrande, spoke with Che in La Higuera shortly before he was killed. He recalled that Che was shot in his right calf, his hair was matted and dirty, his clothes were shredded, and his feet were shod in rough handmade sandals. According to General Nino de Guzman, Che kept his head high, looked everyone in the eye, and asked only for something to smoke. The general told a reporter: "I took pity since he looked so terrible, and gave him my small bag of imported tobacco for his pipe. He smiled and thanked me" (Tamayo 1997). When the Argentine anthropologist

Inchaurregui inspected the jacket dug up next to Che's remains, he found a small bag of pipe tobacco in the inside pocket that had apparently been missed by the soldiers who searched Che's body after he was killed in La Higuera. General Nino de Guzman acknowledged that this was irrefutable evidence the remains were indeed Che's. He told a reporter: "I must tell you I had serious doubts at the beginning. I thought the Cubans would just fi nd any old bones and call it Che. . . . But after hearing about the tobacco pouch, I have no doubts" (Tamayo 1997).

T he Bolivian government gave the Cubans permission to take Che's remains to Cuba along with those of all the other guerrillas who were found buried in unmarked graves in Bolivia, including the bones of Tania (Haydée Tamara Bunke, the only woman in Che's guerrilla force) and Joaquín (Comandante Juan Vitalio Acuña Nuñez, Che's Cuban comrade and the second in command of the guerrilla force). Thus, on October 11, 1997, almost exactly 30 years after Che's death, his remains and those of the other six fallen comrades found buried with him were placed on display in fl ag-draped caskets inside the monument to José Martí in Havana (*Los Angeles Times*, October 12, 1997:A1). With a huge 50-foot mural of Che overlooking the Plaza de la Revolución, hundreds of thousands of Cubans waited in line to pay their respects. After seven days of offi cial mourning and national homage to Che's life and ideals, the caskets were taken to the city of Santa Clara, where Che had led the guerrilla column that scored a decisive victory in the Cuban Revolution. In Santa Clara, Che's coffi n was placed in a newly constructed mausoleum at the base of a large statue of him holding a rifl e in his hand.

At the quasi-religious ceremony held in Santa Clara, and in the presence of Che's widow, Aleida March, their two daughters and their two sons, Fidel Castro praised Che's qualities as the ideal revolutionary. He closed his homage to Che before the assembled crowd with the following words: "Thank you, Che, for your history, your life and your example. Thank you for coming to reinforce us in the diffi cult struggle in which we are engaged today to preserve the ideas for which you fought so hard" (Rother 1997).

In the midst of this massive public veneration of Che, his daughter Aleida Guevara, who is a doctor like her father, told a press conference that her father always shunned public adulation when he was an important public fi gure in Cuba and that he probably would have been embarrassed by all the celebrations in his honor. She also said that it hurt to see the image of her father marketed for commercial purposes on ashtrays, beer, and jeans, but that she hoped some young people would see beyond this commercialism and search for the ideals that her father stood for, especially in a globalized society that is losing all its values (Fineman 1997). Like his older sister, Che's son Camilo Guevara, a lawyer in the Cuban Ministry of Fisheries, is protective of his father's memory and image. He also has criticized what he characterizes as "the bad intentions" of some of the authors of the books published about his father.

Interestingly, in many of the articles published by U.S. newspapers on the return of Che's remains to Cuba and the celebrations that were held in his honor, the reporters used the opportunity to criticize Cuba's socialist system and Che Guevara's ideas on revolution. They characterized them as anachronistic and no longer relevant in the contemporary period. However, the defeat of Che's guerrilla operation in Bolivia does not indicate that an armed revolution is impossible in Latin America. As long as the existing political and economic elites in the region continue to postpone badly needed social and economic reforms and the gap between the rich and the poor continues to increase, popular insurrection will remain on the agenda in Latin America and in other parts of the world with similar conditions. Moreover, the use of repressive and undemocratic measures by those in power to block peaceful and legal efforts to bring about basic economic, political, and social reforms invariably provokes the use of nonpeaceful and extralegal means by those who see they have no other options if they want to create a more just social order.

CHAPTER SIX

Che's Enduring Legacy

C he left an enduring legacy that has grown rather than diminished over the years since his death in 1967. At the public tribute to Che held in the Plaza de la Revolución in Havana following his death in 1967, Fidel Castro (1967) heralded Che's legacy when he said:

If we want a model of a person that does not belong to our time but to the future, I say from the depths of my heart that such a model, without a single stain on his conduct, on his actions, or his behavior, is Che!

Castro anticipated in his speech what has over the years become true: in Cuba and for his many admirers around the world Che has become a heroic model of the totally committed revolutionary, the selfl ess human being who dedicates his life for the common good to bring about a better future for humanity. In socialist Cuba, he is held up as the most outstanding example of the kind of human being Cuba's socialist society is preparing for the 21st century and the socialist future just over the horizon.

M oreover, in the more than four decades that have passed since his death, Che has become an international revolutionary icon, a famous symbol of resistance to social injustice around the world. His romantic image and the revolutionary example he has left behind as his legacy have taken on a transcendent quality that appeals to people in diverse cultures and circumstances. An examination of the reasons for this phenomenon is of considerable importance, since it reveals a great deal about the nature and global signifi cance of Che's enduring legacy.

CHE HAS BECOME A REVOLUTIONARY ICON

Since his death, posters displaying Che's portrait have appeared in almost every major city in the world. The Che on these posters and placards is a heroic fi gure, with the unmistakable beard, beret, and piercing eyes that have come to be associated with this legendary revolutionary. In many of these mass-produced portraits of Che, the heroic face that peers out from them somehow seems to combine in one human countenance all the races of mankind. His eyes and mustache appear Asiatic,

while the darkness of his complexion seems African, and the shape of his nose and cheeks are distinctively European. Perhaps this partially explains why he has become an icon for radical political activists, guerrillas, rebels, leftist students, and intellectuals on every continent, and why, for example, his face is often the only white one to appear alongside those of nonwhite revolutionary heroes in Africa, Asia, and Latin America.

Following his death, in the late 1960s and throughout the 1970s leftist students, radical intellectuals, and revolutionary movements around the world constantly quoted Che's famous dictum "The duty of every revolutionary is to make the revolution." They believed, as did Che, revolutions are made by people who are willing to act, not by those who are waiting for the appropriate objective conditions or for orders from the offi cial Communist Party or the leaders of the Soviet Union or China. It is interesting in this regard to note the offi cial Communist press in the Soviet Union, Eastern Europe, and the People's Republic of China during the 1970s and 1980s often referred to the young leftists in these radical student and political movements as "Guevarist hippies" and "left-wing adventurers." However, such attacks were a matter of little importance to these movements, since they regarded Guevara's activist revolutionary ideas as an alternative to the overly dogmatic and bureaucratic party lines of the more orthodox Communists who were in power in the Soviet Union and China and to the tepid reformism of the moderate socialist and social democratic parties in Western Europe and elsewhere.

Because of his undaunted and fi ercely independent revolutionary idealism, Che became the idol of the New Left during the late 1960s and 1970s in the United States and Great Britain, the bulwarks of capitalism and bourgeois democracy. For a time, students at the London School of Economics and Political Science, one of the most hallowed of Britain's institutions of higher education, greeted each other with the salutation "Che." In the United States, buttons, shirts, placards, and posters with Che's face were present at nearly every antiwar demonstration during the Vietnam War years. Signifi cantly, they have appeared again in the protests against the wars in Iraq and Afghanistan.

In Latin America, where Che gave his life fi ghting for ideals, his name became a battle cry among leftist students, intellectuals, and workers during the 1970s and 1980s. His death at the hands of the

Bolivian army made him an instant martyr for all those who were opposed to the ruling elites and the glaring social injustices that plague this troubled region of the world.

Today, many Latin Americans remember and admire him for his uncompromising revolutionary idealism, his sensitivity to the plight of Latin America's impoverished masses, the rapid worldwide fame he acquired as one of the top leaders of the Cuban government during the heady days following the Cuban Revolution, and his willingness to die fi ghting for the realization of his ideals of social justice, anti-imperialism, and socialism. Che truly belongs in the pantheon of the region's most famous revolutionary leaders—José Martí, Augusto César Sandino, Emiliano Zapata, Pancho Villa, Camilo Torres, and Fidel Castro.

CHE'S LEGACY IN CUBA

I n Cuba, Che holds one of the highest positions in Cuba's pantheon of revolutionary heroes and martyrs. Less than a week after Fidel Castro acknowledged Che had indeed been killed by the Bolivian military, hundreds of thousands of Cubans silently fi lled Havana's Plaza de la Revolución to listen tearfully to Castro as he told dozens of anecdotes about Che and praised Che's outstanding intellectual, political, and military virtues. Backed by a huge portrait of Che and fl anked by Cuban fl ags, Castro gave notice of the importance the Cuban regime would give in the future to Che's revolutionary example. Near the end of his tribute to his fallen comrade, Castro said:

If we ask ourselves how we want our revolutionary fi ghters, our militants, and our people to be, then we must answer without any hesitation: let them be like Che! If we wish to express how we want the people of future generations to be, we must say: let them be like Che! If we ask how we desire to educate our children, we should say without hesitation: we want our children to be educated in the spirit of Che! (Deutschmann 1994:78)

Today, the Cuban regime continues to educate the youth of the country about Che. His picture is in every Cuban school, and Cuba's schoolchildren learn by heart quotations from his writings and his letters. All know the stirring hymn "Seremos como el Che" (We will be like Che), which is sung on many occasions.

S everal generations of Cubans also know this famous paragraph from Che's farewell letter to his children:

Remember that the revolution is what is most important and that each one of us, alone, is worth nothing. Above all, always remain

capable of feeling deeply whatever injustice is committed against anyone in any part of the world. This is the fi nest quality of a revolutionary. (Deutschmann 1997:349)

Part of his legacy is his children. With his fi rst wife, Hilda Gadea, he had a daughter, Hilda Beatriz Guevara Gadea, born February 15, 1956, in Mexico City (she died of cancer August 21, 1995, in Havana, Cuba, at the age of 39). With his second wife, Aleida March, he had four children: Aleida Guevara March, born November 24, 1960, in Havana; Camilo Guevara March, born May 20, 1962, in Havana; Celia Guevara March, born June 14, 1963, in Havana; and Ernesto Guevara March, born February 24, 1965, in Havana.

H is daughter Aleida is a medical doctor and an important Cuban political fi gure in her own right. She represents the family at most public functions. His sons Camilo and Ernesto are lawyers, and his daughter Celia is a veterinarian and marine biologist who works with dolphins and sea lions. Among them they have eight children, Che's grandchildren. It is also rumored Che had another child from an alleged extramarital relationship with Lilia Rosa López, and this child is supposedly Omar Pérez, born in Havana March 19, 1964 (Castañeda 1998:264 – 65).

F or a regime that wishes to instill a revolutionary socialist and internationalist consciousness in its young, there is no better example than Che. His revolutionary ideals and personal example have become part of the social consciousness of several generations of Cubans. And he remains the Cuban model for the 21st-century socialist—"the new human being who is to be glimpsed on the horizon," which he wrote about in his now famous essay "Socialism and Man" (1965).

Elsewhere, Che has also become a pop hero. In the United States, western Europe, and Latin America his image has become commercialized through the marketing of shirts, handkerchiefs, music albums, CD covers, posters, beer, ash trays, jeans, watches, and even towels imprinted with his picture or name. As a pop or commercialized hero fi gure, Che is often depicted in a sardonic or satirical manner. In this commercialized iconic image he is not the heroic revolutionary fi gure the Cuban leaders and his contemporary admirers hold up as the model of the 21stcentury human being; rather, he is a humorous or satirical caricature. For his family and friends as well as those who admire Che as a heroic revolutionary, the use of his famous image to market products in the capitalist marketplace is just as denigrating as the image of Che held by his avowed enemies, who regard him as a fanatical killer, a psychopath, or a sinister Communist renegade.

T he phenomenon of hero worship and the process by which individuals become popular heroes have always been something of a mystery. In all times and places there appears to be a need for heroes. However, in times of great change, this need seems greatest. Today, people around the globe see their societies and humanity in general undergoing far-reaching changes. Many fi nd their lives adversely affected by these changes and are frightened about the future that these changes may bring, while others hope for signifi cant improvements in society and the quality of their own lives through radical changes in the existing order. Both groups appear to need the assurance that human beings can control their fate and shape the future according to their desires. They sometimes fi nd this assurance in the words and deeds of an exceptional individual, whose courage and individual efforts to shape the future according to his or her ideals, even if seemingly unsuccessful, give them inspiration. This appears to be one of the reasons Che continues to be such a popular hero.

C he had the courage to act in accordance with his ideals. He gave his life fi ghting for a brave new world that he believed he could help bring into being. It is little wonder he is admired for this. As a Latin American Catholic priest I met in Bolivia said shortly after Che's death: "To pass one's life in the jungle, ill clothed and starving, with a price on his head, confronting the military power of imperialism, and on top of that, sick with asthma, exposing himself to death by suffocation if the bullets did not cut him down fi rst, a man, who could have lived regally, with money, amusements, friends, women, and vices in any of the great cities of sin; this is heroism, true heroism, no matter how confused or wrong his ideas might have been. Not to recognize this is not only reactionary, but stupid."

C he's exceptional devotion to the realization of his ideals was truly heroic, and indeed it would be foolish not to recognize this. Those who recognize the heroism in his character and actions cannot help admiring Che, regardless of whether they agree with his revolutionary politics and utopian ideals. Che continues to be a hero for all those who admire and are inspired by his idealism and his exceptional human courage.

EL HOMBRE NUEVO —THE NEW HUMAN BEING

Che's vision of the new human being (*el hombre nuevo*) inspired not only him and his comrades but also the young Bolivian revolutionaries who followed in his footsteps a few years after his death. After escaping the Bolivian military's efforts to hunt down the last survivors of Che's guerrilla force, Inti Peredo and Darío (a Bolivian whose real name was David Adriazola) went into hiding in the jungles of northern Bolivia. There they organized another guerrilla force to continue the struggle initiated by Che (Siles del Valle 1996:38 – 40). However, this guerrilla force was short lived and in 1969 both Inti and Darío were caught and killed in the Bolivian capital city of La Paz. Thus, they too sacrifi ced their lives fi ghting, like Che and their former comrades, for a new society and a new kind of human being.

During this period, Che's concept of *el hombre nuevo* and many of his other revolutionary ideals found sympathy among many of the adherents of an unorthodox Christian body of theory and practice know as Liberation Theology (Boff and Boff 1988). In the 1960s and 1970s, this body of socially concerned and unorthodox religious views gained signifi cant support among the more progressive elements of the Catholic Church in Latin America. Many of its adherents established close links with the revolutionary movements in the region. And in some cases the most progressive sectors of the Church, infl uenced by the ideals of Liberation Theology, joined radical Marxist and neo-Marxist political movements in Bolivia and in other countries such as Chile, Peru, Brazil, Nicaragua, El Salvador, and Guatemala.

After the deaths of Inti Peredo and Darío, this convergence of views resulted in the participation of some of the younger members of Bolivia's Christian Democratic Party in a revolutionary guerrilla movement that called itself the Ejército de Liberación Nacional (National Liberation Army), the same name used by Che's group. This movement was led by none other than Osvaldo "Chato" Peredo, the younger brother of Inti and Coco Peredo (Siles del Valle 1996:40 – 43). In 1970 this movement attempted to establish a guerrilla foco near the mining town of Teoponte, north of the capital of La Paz. They were quickly surrounded and defeated by the Bolivian army, and in a totally unnecessary act of brutality many of them were massacred by the army after they offered to surrender. Only a few survived, largely as a result of the intervention of the local leaders of the Catholic Church. Chato Peredo, who is now a psychotherapist in La Paz, was one of the few survivors who were imprisoned and later released (Anderson 1997:745).

A fter the massacre by the Bolivian army of most of the young participants in the Teoponte guerrilla foco, an important change began to take place in Bolivian popular culture and politics. Although the idea of guerrilla warfare was rejected as a viable form of resistance to the military regime, important elements within Bolivian society began to idealize and even venerate Che and the other fallen guerrillas as martyrs (Siles del Valle 1996:44 – 45). Che's death, his concept of the new human being, the ideals of Liberation Theology, the deaths of so many idealistic young Bolivians in the revolutionary movements inspired by Che and his comrades—all these elements combined to exert a major infl uence on Bolivian popular culture, literature, and politics that has continued to this day. It is even possible to speak today of the sanctifi cation of the guerrillas in the minds of many people in Bolivia.

SIGNIFICANCE AND EFFECTS OF CHE'S FAILED BOLIVIAN MISSION

I ndeed, the death of Che Guevara and the failure of his guerrilla operation in Bolivia have not stopped attempts to bring about meaningful change in the region through armed revolution. In fact, Che's failure helped to clarify what is needed to organize a successful armed insurrection against an unjust and oppressive regime. Subsequent revolutionary movements have appeared in Latin America and in other parts of the world since Che's death, and in most cases they have taken into account the importance of mobilizing mass political support for their movements in urban as well as rural areas.

The revolutionary movements that occurred in Central America during the late 1970s and 1980s were founded on this approach. Since the 1990s the Zapatista revolutionary movement in southern Mexico, described in chapter 6, and the Bolivarian revolution in Venezuela (led by that country's leftist president Hugo Chávez Frías) have been based on mass political support organized in both urban and rural areas. Signifi cantly, they frequently give homage to Che's revolutionary legacy.

C he's failed mission in Bolivia proved, among other things, that a well-trained and committed revolutionary guerrilla force is not suffi cient to detonate a successful revolution. Che's Bolivian operation demonstrated that unless an armed movement mobilizes popular support among the middle and working classes in urban areas as well as poorer sectors of the rural population it will be isolated and wiped out by government troops using what are now commonly understood counterinsurgency tactics. In other words, the creation of a popular-based, multiclass revolutionary movement is widely regarded today as the basic prerequisite for a successful popular revolution. It is, of course, far more diffi cult to create than a guerrilla foco in a relatively isolated rural area, but it is not outside the realm of possibility in the present global order. In fact, this type of popular-based revolutionary movement has emerged in recent years in various parts of the world (in Latin America, the Middle East, Africa, and Asia) and will surely emerge again in the near future.

As the preceding discussion seeks to make clear, Che's death and the failure of his guerrilla operation in Bolivia have enriched the international pool of revolutionary theory and practice. The lessons learned from the failure of his movement have led many revolutionary or rebellious political and social groups around the world to develop more successful strategies for gaining power. Moreover, as a result of Che's willingness to die for his revolutionary ideals and his martyrdom in the pursuit of these ideals, he has become a universal model of revolutionary courage and commitment, and his example continues to inspire new generations of revolutionaries and leftist political activists around the world.

More than four decades have passed since Che Guevara was killed in the little village of La Higuera in Bolivia. However, the social injustices against which this famous revolutionary fought—fi rst in the Cuban revolution, then in the Congo, and fi nally in Bolivia—are very much in existence today. For this reason, Che's revolutionary life and death continue to inspire those who struggle against these injustices, particularly in Latin America.

C he's revolutionary legacy can be found in the words and deeds of workers, poor peasants, middle-class university students, intellectuals, shantytown dwellers, the leaders of indigenous communities, and the landless and the homeless —from the tip of Argentina to Mexico's border with the United States, from the Andean valleys of Peru and Bolivia to the cities and vast Amazonian region of Brazil, and of course everywhere in Cuba. Che is the focus of hundreds of books and articles, as well as fi lms, paintings, sculptures, and murals, in Europe, North America, South America, Africa, and Asia. Today his face and name are known throughout the world, and his revolutionary legacy has acquired an enduring global signifi cance. In particular, the shift to the left in contemporary Latin American politics has created renewed interest in Che's revolutionary ideals, his struggle against social injustice and his dedication to the revolutionary unifi cation of Latin America.

As his fi rst wife, Hilda Gadea (2008:21–22), wrote in her book about Che, for many people around the world he is the "exemplary revolutionary" and "a man of principle whose true understanding is essential to the struggle for justice in Latin America and other parts of the world."

They see him as an "example for the young generation of the Americas and the world" to follow because of "his faith in mankind, his love for the dispossessed, and his total commitment to the struggle against exploitation and poverty."

CHAPTER SEVEN

!Che Vive!_Che's Continuing Influence in Latin America

I n Latin America, Che is as politically important today as he was when he died in Bolivia over four decades ago. In some ways he is even more important now. In recent years there has been a dramatic shift to the left in the politics of most Latin American countries. This shift in the political orientation of this important region of the world has given rise to renewed interest in Che Guevara's ideals of Pan-American unity, antiimperialism, and humanist socialism.

T his rather remarkable change of direction in the region's politics is largely in response to the failure of the neoliberal agenda of free-market and free-trade capitalism pursued by the U.S. government, the International Monetary Fund, the World Bank, the Inter-American Development Bank, and most of the governments of the region since the 1980s. The neoliberal economic and social policies promoted by these Washington-based institutions (often referred to as the Washington Consensus) have widened the gap between the rich and the poor, while they have denationalized the economies and privatized the governments of most of the countries in the region. The tidal wave of popular opposition to these neoliberal policies and to the adverse effects of the accompanying globalization of these societies (i.e., the denationalization of their economies so that they can be more effectively integrated into the expanding global capitalist system) has generated new political movements and new populist leaders who openly identify with Che Guevara's ideals and his revolutionary struggle.

CHE AND CONTEMPORARY BOLIVIAN POLITICS

T here is no better example of Che's infl uence than Bolivia. After suffering for decades under U.S.-backed right-wing governments, which imposed neoliberal policies that adversely affected the majority of the population, the country's largely indigenous population has risen up in opposition and found its political voice. The political mobilization of the poor majority of the country led to the election in the fall of 2005 of Bolivia's leftist president Juan "Evo" Morales, who won the election with some 54 percent of the votes. Popularly known as Evo, he is of indigenous descent (Aymará) and is the leader of the Movimiento al Socialismo (MAS, or Movement toward Socialism). As previously mentioned in chapter 11, Antonio Peredo—the oldest brother of Coco, Inti, and Chato Peredo— and Loyola Guzman, who was a member of the urban support network for Che's guerrilla force in Bolivia, are prominent members of MAS, as are many other leftist intellectuals, workers, and peasants in Bolivia.

Morales is the fi rst person from Bolivia's indigenous majority to lead the country since the Spanish conquest subjugated the indigenous population 500 years ago. He and the other leaders of MAS are outspoken admirers of Che Guevara. They have placed photos of Che in the national parliament building and a portrait of Che made from local coca leaves in the presidential offi ces. The MAS-led government has initiated a constitutional revision of the country's governmental system, an agrarian reform program, and nationalization of the country's mining and natural gas industries. Thus, the Morales government is reversing the direction of Bolivia's economic, social, and political development. Instead of privatization of public services and denationalization of the economy, the country's new leadership is committed to regaining national control over the country's mining and natural gas industries and using the revenues from these industries to fi nance a people-centered, equitable, and environmentally sustainable program of social and economic development.

Before his offi cial inauguration as president of Bolivia on January 22, 2006, Morales went to the archaeological site and spiritual center of Tiwanaku, the capital of one of the most ancient cultures in the world, where he was crowned the honorary supreme leader of the Aymará and was given gifts from representatives of indigenous peoples from all over the Americas. In the speech that he gave at the La Puerta del Sol, or the Door of the Sun, which is the gateway into the ancient temple of Kalasasaya, Morales said that "the struggle that Che Guevara left uncompleted, we shall complete" (Granma January 23, 2006). Afterward, in the speech he gave at his inauguration, he included Che among the fallen heroes in the 500-year struggle of his people for their freedom.

E ven more signifi cant is that Morales went to La Higuera, where Che was killed, to celebrate Che's 78th birthday on June 14, 2006. He is the fi rst Bolivian head of state to have ever visited the village and he chose this date to pay tribute to Che, to offi cially open the medical center the government of Cuba donated to the village, and to congratulate the local graduates of the literacy program Yes I Can, which has been advised and equipped by the Cuban government. Che's son Camilo Guevara was present as well as the Cuban ambassador to Bolivia and a number of Cuban doctors in their white coats. Morales pledged Bolivia's solidarity with Cuba and Venezuela and said he would be willing to take up arms to defend them if they are attacked by the United States (Delacour 2006). Hugo Moldiz, a journalist who is the coordinator of the political front of some 30 different popular organizations that support Morales's government, told the press that the medical clinic and the literacy program demonstrated the relevance of Che's revolutionary struggle, since one of the reasons he gave his life fi ghting in Bolivia was to ensure that the Bolivian people had access to adequate health care and education (Mayoral and González 2006).

A ccompanied by Bolivian government offi cials and the Cuban ambassador, President Morales also went to inaugurate the installation of modern medical equipment at the Vallegrande hospital—the same hospital where Che was last seen before his body was secretly buried near the airstrip in Vallegrande. Today, the laundry building where Che's body was laid out for examination and where the last photos were taken of

him has become a shrine in his memory. Morales's visit to La Higuera and Vallegrande as the Bolivian head of state is the fi rst time that any high government offi cial in

Bolivia has paid tribute to Che Guevara and his guerrilla mission in Bolivia. Moldiz, who has close ties to Cuba, told the press that Morales's tribute to Che was consistent with the path of Morales's own struggle and with the identifi cation of his government with the ideals of Che.

CHE AND CONTEMPORARY POLITICS IN VENEZUELA AND ECUADOR

Che's ideas about the need to create new human beings guided by socialist morality and his critique of bureaucratism have found particular resonance in Venezuela today (Munckton 2007). The regime of Hugo Chávez has widely distributed copies of the critical essay Che wrote on bureaucratism while he was a minister in the Cuban government. But even though Chávez has pointed to Cuba as an important source of inspiration, he has emphasized that Venezuela will have to create its own form of socialism to fi t its particular history and conditions. The emphasis on direct democracy in Venezuela is consistent with this perspective, and Chávez contends that the only way to overcome poverty is to give power to the poor. Thus, he and his supporters contend that the Bolivarian revolution will create a democratic, humanist socialism rather than the bureaucratic, authoritarian style of so-called socialism that existed in the Soviet Union. It is in this context that Che's revolutionary legacy has found the most fertile soil in Venezuela and Bolivia today. His writings, his deeds in the Cuban Revolution and his personal sacrifi ce in the struggle for human liberation and social justice are a source of great inspiration and guidance to the Venezuelans and the Bolivians who are struggling for these same ideals today.

I n Ecuador, Che is also held in high esteem. Much like Chávez and Morales, the country's new leftist president Rafael Correa Delgado laced his acceptance speech on January 15, 2007, with references to Simón Bolívar and Che Guevara. He said his country needs to build a 21stcentury socialism to overcome the poverty, inequality, and political instability that have plagued the Ecuadorian people. Both Chávez and Morales were special guests at Correa's inauguration. With them at his side, Correa said: "Latin America isn't living an era of changes"; rather, "it's living a change of eras" and "the long night of neoliberalism is coming to an end" (Fertl 2007). Che would have been happy indeed to hear what Correa said afterward. He said: "A sovereign, dignifi ed, just and socialist Latin America is beginning to rise." Exactly the kind of language Che used four decades earlier.

CHE'S CONTEMPORARY POPULARITY OUTSIDE LATIN AMERICA

C ritical observers of Che's contemporary popularity in North America, Europe, and other regions outside Latin America are quick to point out that his iconic image has become a global brand, often devoid of any ideological or political signifi cance when it is used to market certain products. They dismiss his continuing appeal to youth as merely a case of "adolescent revolutionary romanticism" and radical chic (O'Hagan 2004). However, while it is true Che's image has become quite profi table and is used to market a wide variety of goods to young people in the United States and elsewhere, his image still has political signifi cance. Consequently, his image was removed from a CD carrying case recently in the United States after it sparked signifi cant criticism in the media, in which Che was compared with Osama bin Laden and Adolf Hitler (Reyes 2006). Target Corporation, the large retail company that distributed the product in question, felt compelled to withdraw it from sale and issue a public apology for selling the item. This incident is proof that Che's supposedly apolitical iconic image still has too much political signifi cance for many shoppers in the global capitalist shopping mall.

Moreover, even in the United States, the center of global capitalism, Che still fi nds political admirers. When asked several years ago why his father is perceived as a devil by American corporations and believers in the free market, Che's son Camilo accurately pointed out that "he is a devil for the U.S. government and American multinationals" but that "many North Americans admire and respect El Che" and "they fi ght injustice in American society under his banner" (HUMO 1998). Thus, one sees Che Guevara images along the U.S.-Mexico border as manifestations of activism. Although Che Guevara was not Mexican, his image has been appropriated by activists in the Mexican community within the United States who seek more access to education and civil rights, and the use of his image can be seen as a critique of current U.S. immigration policy. Camilo also correctly noted that there are people in the United

States who declare their solidarity with Cuba and seek to lift the U.S. economic blockade against his country.

P rominent public intellectuals such as Régis Debray in France, Jorge Castañeda in Mexico, Alvaro Vargas Llosa in Peru (son of the famous novelist Mario Vargas Llosa), Pacho O'Donnell in Argentina, and others have done their best to demystify and dismiss the signifi cance of the enduring popularity of Che, particularly among young people. One of the most representative members of this group of critics is the British-born liberal savant Christopher Hitchens, who supported the Cuban revolution in the 1960s but has since called himself a recovering Marxist. In a 1997 review article of Jon Lee Anderson's biography of Che and Che's posthumously published *The Motorcycle Diaries* Hitchens argued that Che's enduring popularity is a contemporary case of classic romantic idolatry. In what has become a familiar argument among intellectuals in the United States and Europe for dismissing Che's iconic popularity, Hitchens asserts that "Che's iconic status was assured because he failed. His story was one of defeat and isolation, and that's why it is so seductive. Had he lived, the myth of Che would have long since died" (Hitchens 1997).

Thus, Hitchens and other intellectuals who share his perspective claim Che "belongs more to the romantic tradition than the revolutionary one," since "to endure as a romantic icon, one must not just die young, but die hopelessly" and, according to Hitchens, "Che fulfi ls both criteria." However, there is a fundamental factual inaccuracy and a false premise in this thesis. Che did not die young. Someone who dies at 39 is hardly young (except to those over 50). His death was untimely to be sure, but he was not young when he died. Furthermore, Hitchens and the other intellectual demystifi ers of Che's iconic popularity fail to comprehend the continuing political and ideological signifi cance of his iconic legacy.

The waving banners, the graffi ti on the walls, the posters, the T-shirts, the videos, the fi lms, the books, the pamphlets, the photos, the songs, the tattoos, and the cries of "¡Che Vive!" on the lips of people around the world provide overwhelming evidence that Che Guevara represents a powerful symbol of one of the most outstanding examples in modern history of resistance to injustice, inequality, exploitation, and political domination. And this is true for people literally around the world. Che continues to be a popular hero for many people—of all ages—for the same reason that Bolivia's President Evo Morales, in his late 40s, says he admires Che: "I admire Che because he fought for equality and for justice," and "he did not just care for ordinary people, he made their struggle his own" (Rieff 2005).

A s art historian Trisha Ziff has astutely noted: "Che's iconic image mysteriously reappears whenever there's a confl ict over injustice [and] there isn't anything else in history that serves in this way" (Lotz 2006). More than anything else, as Ziff acknowledges, Che is a symbol of opposition to imperialism and "in the end, you cannot take this meaning out of the image." Ziff is correct in asserting that the meaning of Che's image is that of the *guerrillero heroico*— the heroic guerrilla fi ghter against imperialism, and particularly U.S. imperialism.

CHE'S INFLUENCE ON CONTEMPORARY LATIN AMERICAN POLITICS

B ut in contemporary Latin America, Che is more than a powerful symbol of resistance to U.S. imperialism; his values and many of his ideas continue to be extremely relevant to the current political reality and the shift to the left in Latin American politics. His views and revolutionary life are fi nding increasing resonance among the new political leaders, new political movements, and rank-and-fi le political activists in the region. They fi nd Che's vision of a socialist future and his ideas about how to get there to be directly relevant to their efforts to end the region's tragic pathology of distorted, neocolonial, and unequal development. Che's ideals and vision of a united, free, and socialist Latin America are a source of inspiration for their pursuit of emancipatory, equitable, and sustainable alternatives to the disempowering, inequitable, and unsustainable structures and values of 21st-century global capitalism. Che is much more than a popular symbol of uncompromising defi ance to injustice and imperial domination; his revolutionary vision of the future and ideas about how to wage the struggle to get there are relevant to the contemporary efforts being made to bring about a revolutionary transformation of the basic economic, political, and social structures in Latin America and the Caribbean.

A s a sign of how times have changed in the region, a little more than a month after President Evo Morales paid a historic tribute to Che Guevara in La Higuera and Vallegrande, a similar unprecedented event took place in nearby Argentina. It will most likely become a legend of its own. Following an important meeting in Córdoba, Argentina, of the MERCOSUR (Southern Common Market) to which Cuba was invited and Venezuela was accepted as a new member, Hugo Chávez and Fidel Castro made a historic pilgrimage to Alta Gracia to tour Che's boyhood home (*Adn mundo.com* 2006).

S ince 2001 the middle-class house, now called Villa Nydia, where Che lived as a boy has served as a museum dedicated to his memory. On July 22, 2006, almost four decades after Che's death, two of the most important heads of state in Latin America paid a highly publicized visit to Che's boyhood home. When they arrived, the waiting crowd of several thousand people responded with a chorus of chants: "Fidel, Fidel, Hugo, Hugo" and "¡Se siente! ¡Se siente! ¡Guevara está presente!"—"One feels it! One feels it! Guevara is present!" (Rey 2006).

As they emerged from their vehicles, the two heads of state waved to the crowd and stopped at the entrance to the house in front of a bronze statue of Che modeled after a photograph taken when he was eight years old. They admired the statue and then went inside for an emotional encounter with the memorabilia of Che's boyhood and family life. Castro was surprised to learn that Che's parents rented the house, and he asked how much rent they had paid (*Adnmundo.com* 2006). When the director of the museum said she really didn't know, Castro jokingly reproached her for not knowing this important fact. At one point, Castro broke down and cried in front of a large picture of Che's mother Celia with her young children around her, including the young Che. Then, Castro and Chávez met with some of Che's childhood friends who were waiting in the house, including Calica Ferrer, who accompanied Che on his trip to Bolivia and Peru in 1953. Castro and Chávez viewed Che's birth certifi cate, handwritten letters, and a motorbike like the one he rode around Argentina. Ariel Vidoza, a childhood friend of Che, answered some of Castro's questions about Che's childhood. Among the answers she gave, she said: "Ernesto didn't like the rich much. He preferred to play with us, the poor ones" (Rey 2006).

As they left the house they posed for photographs with Che's boyhood friends in front of the statue of the young Ernesto. To the reporters waiting outside, Chávez said with a great deal of emotion in his voice: "I came to feed my soul. I am leaving with the batteries of my soul charged for 80 more years of revolutionary struggle and battles" (Venezolana de Televisión 2006). With tears in his eyes, Castro told the reporters and the crowd that he was sorry he and Chávez could not stay longer and waved to the onlookers, who were clapping and cheering.

N o one could possibly have imagined such an event 40 years ago, even 10 years ago. It was a historic scene: Che's comrade in arms, the famous 20th-century revolutionary leader Fidel Castro (80 years old at the time), and Hugo Chávez, one of Latin America's new 21st-century revolutionary leaders, standing shoulder to shoulder in front of Che's boyhood home, which is now a museum of the revolutionary life of the legendary Che Guevara. There they stood in Alta Gracia (High Grace), Argentina, surrounded by a cheering crowd of thousands in Che's homeland, where not too many years earlier a bloody military dictatorship had ruthlessly disappeared anyone thought to be sympathizers of Guevara and Castro.

As the caravan of cars carrying Fidel Castro and Hugo Chávez left Alta Gracia for Córdoba, they passed a building in Che's hometown where someone had written on the wall in bold red letters: "¡Che Vive!" (Che Lives!) There are similar Che Vive slogans on the walls of the laundry building in Vallegrande, Bolivia, where Che's half-nude body was displayed after he was killed over 40 years ago (O'Hagan 2004). What the visit of Fidel Castro and Hugo Chávez to Che's boyhood home in Alta Gracia, Ecuadorian President Correa's televised comments, and the Che Vive slogans on walls in many parts of Latin America and the world refl ect is what his wife, Aleida March, wrote in her foreword to Che's Congo diary (Guevara, March, and Gott 2000:l): "Men do not die when their life and example can serve as a guide to others, and when those others succeed in continuing their work."